Date Due

		JUN	2004
		JUL	09
		JUL	X X 2015

PRINTED IN U.S.A.

HOWELLS, JAMES, BRYANT AND OTHER ESSAYS

BY

WILLIAM LYON PHELPS

KENNIKAT PRESS
Port Washington, New York

HOWELLS, JAMES, BRYANT AND OTHER ESSAYS

Reissued in 1965 by Kennikat Press

Library of Congress Catalog Card No: 65-18609

Manufactured in U. S. A. by Arno Press, Inc.

Indexed in the ESSAY AND GENERAL LITERATURE INDEX

CONTENTS

LIST OF ILLUSTRATIONS

WILLIAM CULLEN BRYANT

BRYANT

William Cullen Bryant was born in the Berkshires, in Western Massachusetts, at a small town called Cummington, on the third of November 1794. His mother was a descendant of John Alden. She possessed a singular nerve, without the plural, as will appear from the following extracts taken from her diary. "Nov. 3, 1794.—Stormy, wind N. E. Churned. Seven in the evening a son born." "Nov. 5, 1794.—Clear, wind N. W. Made Austin a coat. Sat up all day. Went into the kitchen." The poet came from a hardy race.

At the age of ten, he wrote verses, and his first book was published in 1808, when he was thirteen. It is no sign of greatness to compose rimes at an early age, as I have the best of all reasons to believe. Bryant's boyish verses show a correct ear, good technique, and rather remarkable facility.

In 1810, he entered the sophomore class at Williams College. The opportunities for education were not very extensive in the comparatively new institution, and when his roommate transferred to Yale, Bryant naturally wished to accompany him thither. He obtained his father's consent, and spent the summer vacation preparing himself to enter the Junior Class at New Haven. But at the last moment his father informed him that there was not money enough, and the boy's college days came to an end. Bryant always regretted this, but Yale has regretted it even more, as any university would be proud to have his name among its graduates. What effect, if any, further education at that time would have had upon his poetry, may be left to the consideration of those who delight to answer vain questions.

He took up the study of law, and in 1815 became a practicing attorney. It was during these early years of professional work, that he wrote some of his best poetry. On the fifteenth of December 1815, he took a long walk, and after sunset saw a waterfowl against the fading sky. This sight appealed to his imagination, and he wrote the eight stanzas

To a Waterfowl, which many believe to be his masterpiece. It is said that Matthew Arnold declared *To a Waterfowl* to be the best short poem ever written in English. I cannot believe that Matthew Arnold ever said anything quite so foolish as that. There must have been some error in reporting his opinion. The poem is fine both in thought and expression; but it is not a work of genius, and does not approach the masterpieces of the chief English poets.

In 1821 Bryant was happily married, and in 1824 he "abandoned the law for literature," a phrase that occurs with frequency in the biographies of men of letters. The law has always been a favourite choice with young men who do not know what they want, but who know what they do not want. As it is so often selected by a process of elimination, it is not surprising that it is so often "abandoned." Clergymen and physicians usually remain true to their original choice, because the original choice was positive.

In 1825 Bryant moved to New York to enter journalism, and soon became an editor of *The Evening Post,* and in 1828 editor-in-chief. For fifty years he gave himself to this excellent newspaper. He made six journeys to Europe, where he was usually homesick, and yet returned again eagerly. In Hawthorne's *Note-Books,* there is a delightful account of an evening at Casa Guidi in Florence, where Robert Browning, Elizabeth Barrett Browning, William Cullen Bryant and Nathaniel Hawthorne ate strawberries and discussed spiritualism. Hawthorne speaks of Bryant's hoary beard and calm dignity, and says that he and Browning were polite to each other, though it was his (Hawthorne's) opinion that neither cared anything for the other's poetry, which was probably a true observation.

Bryant died in 1878, at the age of eighty-three, vigorous and busy to the very last.

Few writers have had a longer literary career than Bryant. The dates of his first and of his last published book have between them seventy years, from 1808 to 1878. Perhaps it seems even more impressive when we remember that Bryant published poetry during the administration of Thomas Jefferson and of Rutherford B. Hayes.

The amount of his production is in inverse

proportion to the opportunity. His career was astonishingly long, his output astonishingly small. He was the exception that proves the rule; for in his case we might with accuracy reverse the proverb, and say that life was long and art was short. Shelley, Bryant, and Keats were all born about the same time, but there the resemblance stops.

Shelley, born 1792; died 1822.
Keats, born 1795; died 1821.
Bryant, born 1794; died 1878.

Keats's poetical career lasted three years—he produced considerably more than Bryant. Shelley's career lasted twelve years—he produced three times as much as Bryant. Ordinarily the two Englishmen would have shown quality, and the American quantity; but the two excelled in both.

I think it should always be accounted unto Bryant for righteousness, that he permitted so small an amount of his production to appear in print. He had no illusions about himself; and he had an immense respect for the art of poetry. That he should have published his first book at the age of thirteen, should have lived to be eighty-three, and then have been able to include all his original poems in one smallish volume, is sufficient evidence of his modesty.

Thanatopsis is undoubtedly a great poem. But it is not a precocious poem, nor was it, as it is now universally printed, written by Bryant in extreme youth. I suppose there is no important poem in literature whose origin and first publication are enveloped in so dense a fog of error.

The late Thomas Wentworth Higginson, in his *History of American Literature,* says of Bryant, "His merely boyish poems . . . the *Thanatopsis,* in particular, written at seventeen,—have perhaps never been equalled in literature by any boy of that age." No part of the above statement is accurate; and it contains three important errors. The *Thanatopsis* is not a boyish poem; it was not, in anything like its present form, written at seventeen; and in its original publication, it has been surpassed by many poets at an even earlier age.

Other well-printed and nicely-bound Histories of American Literature contain the following statements: *Thanatopsis* was written in 1816; in 1811; was first published in

1816; in 1814. Bryant himself said he did not know when it was written.

Thanatopsis was first published in the *North American Review* for September 1817. Bryant was then nearly twenty-three years old, which is not young for a genius. But, as printed in the *Review* it is very far from being a masterpiece, juvenile or otherwise; the best part of *Thanatopsis,* as we know it today, was not included, for the simple reason that it had not yet been written; and in its place appeared lines that are banal.

Not a word of the following splendid introduction appears in the original printed version:

To him who in the love of Nature holds
Communion with her visible forms, she speaks
A various language; for his gayer hours
She has a voice of gladness, and a smile
And eloquence of beauty, and she glides
Into his darker musings, with a mild
And healing sympathy, that steals away
Their sharpness, ere he is aware. When thoughts
Of the last bitter hour come like a blight
Over thy spirit, and sad images
Of the stern agony, and shroud, and pall,
And breathless darkness, and the narrow house,
Make thee to shudder, and grow sick at heart;—
Go forth, under the open sky, and list

To Nature's teachings, while from all around—
Earth and her waters, and the depths of air—
Comes a still voice—

The noble, stately, solemn conclusion is also missing:

So live, that when thy summons comes to join
The innumerable caravan, which moves
To that mysterious realm, where each shall take
His chamber in the silent halls of death,
Thou go not, like the quarry-slave at night,
Scourged to his dungeon, but, sustained and soothed
By an unfaltering trust, approach thy grave,
Like one who wraps the drapery of his couch
About him, and lies down to pleasant dreams.

Furthermore, some of the best lines in the body of the poem were not added till later. For example:

Old Ocean's gray and melancholy waste,

Instead of the lines

The gay will laugh
When thou art gone

the original version has the unfortunate

The tittering world
Dance to the grave.

Instead of the sublime introductory lines, the poem as first published in 1817, began with the following four stanzas, which make their acceptance difficult to understand, and the enthusiasm of the editor incomprehensible.

Not that from life, and all its woes
The hand of death shall set me free;
Not that this head, shall then repose
In the low vale most peacefully.

Ah, when I touch time's farthest brink,
A kinder solace must attend;
It chills my very soul, to think
On that dread hour when life must end.

In vain the flatt'ring verse may breathe,
Of ease from pain, and rest from strife,
There is a sacred dread of death
Inwoven with the strings of life.

This bitter cup at first was given
When angry *justice* frown'd severe,
And 'tis the eternal doom of heaven
That man must view the grave with fear.

—Yet a few days, and then, etc.

Four years later, in 1821, Bryant published a volume of poems. He was then twenty-seven years old. In this volume, *Thanatopsis,* except in some minor details, appeared in the form now familiar to us all. He was certainly a good critic of his own work, and knew how to improve it, yes, how to transform it. It is this book, the *Poems* of 1821, that marks the birth of American poetry.

But although *Thanatopsis* shows no precocity, Bryant was a precocious poet, one of the most remarkable on record. In April 1808, when he was thirteen, he wrote a longish poem, called *The Embargo*. At that time Pope was still the reigning influence on New England verse, and the boy Bryant followed him not only in satirical content, but in the metrically monotonous heroic couplet. *The Embargo* was a Federalist satire on the policy of President Jefferson, for at that time Bryant was a zealous Federalist rather eager for secession; later he became an uncompromising Democrat, and admired the statesman he had originally condemned. Perhaps this is one reason why Bryant was afterwards ashamed of this early work, and did not like to hear it mentioned.

The Embargo was published in the same year of its composition, 1808, and went into a second edition in 1809. It is a bibliographical curiosity, much sought after by collectors. Mr. Andrew Keogh, the Yale University Librarian, furnishes me with the following information:

The first edition of *The Embargo* was a pamphlet of twelve pages in marbled paper covers, measuring less than 5 by 8 inches. It was anonymous, the title reading: *The Embargo, or Sketches of the Times; a Satire. By a youth of thirteen. Boston: Printed for the subscribers.* Only four or five copies are known, and only two have been sold by auction within the last forty years. In 1877 a copy was sold at the Hoffman sale in New York for $17, and found its way into the library of General Rush C. Hawkins of New York. At the sale of his library ten years later, it was bought by Mr. Hoe of New York for $41.50, and at the Hoe sale in April, 1911, it was bought by Mr. Walter T. Wallace of New York for $3,350. The Hoe copy was beautifully bound in red levant morocco by Alfred Mathews, but Mr. Wallace wanted one in the original marbled wrappers, so when such a copy appeared in a New York auction in December, 1912, he bought it for $3,000.

The Alldis collection in the Yale University Library contains a copy of the second edition, from which I transcribe the following preliminary *Advertisement:*

A doubt having been intimated in the Monthly Anthology of June last, whether a youth of thirteen years could have been the author of this poem —in justice to his merits the friends of the writer feel obliged to certify the fact from their personal knowledge of himself and his family, as well as his literary improvement and extraordinary talents. They would premise, that they do not come uncalled before the public, to bear this testimony—they would prefer that he should be judged by his works, without favour or affection. As the doubt has been suggested, they deem it merely an act of justice to remove it—after which they leave him a candidate for favour in common with other literary adventurers. They, therefore, assure the public, that Mr. Bryant, the author, is a native of Cummington, in the county of Hampshire, and in the month of November last arrived at the age of fourteen years. The facts can be authenticated by many of the inhabitants of that place, as well as by several of his friends who give this notice; and if it be deemed worthy of further inquiry, the printer is enabled to disclose their names and places of residence.

February, 1809.

That the thirteen year old political thinker was not lacking in assurance may be seen from the following lines in his poem, in which he demands Thomas Jefferson's immediate resignation:

Go, wretch, resign the presidential chair,
Disclose thy secret measures, foul or fair.

Go, search with curious eye, for horned frogs,
Mid the wild wastes of Louisianian bogs;
Or, where Ohio rolls his turbid stream,
Dig for huge bones, thy glory and thy theme.

The last four lines were intended to ridicule Jefferson's interest in natural history. The reference to Belgium was unconsciously prophetic of certain events in the twentieth century:

Aspiring Belgia, once the patriot's pride
When barbarous Alva, her brave sons defied;
The nurse of arts, th' advent'rous merchant's boast,
Whose wide-spread commerce whiten'd every coast.
Humbled, degraded, by the vilest arts,
Beneath his iron scourge, succumbing smarts;
The crowded city, the canal's green shore,
Fair haunts of free-born opulence, no more!

Although Bryant worked in a newspaper office in New York for fifty years, the city made little impression either on his character or his manners. He was never urban, like Irving or Willis. He was not clubable. He carried the New England winter not only in his beard, but in his mind. There was a certain austerity in his bearing, that in milder moments took on the aspect of dignified serenity, and at other times was akin to gruff ness. He loved old things and old ways; he always wrote with a quill, "which he sharpened with a knife as old as himself." A good deal of reserve characterised his poetry, which at its warmest never reached the boiling point. This may partly have been owing to the fact that when he was a child, his parents, becoming alarmed at the unnaturally large size of his head, used to soak it in cold water, sometimes breaking the ice to do so. Bryant never quite got this chill out of his style.

Bryant's father was a Unitarian, but his mother brought the boy up in the Calvinistic faith, which he soon abandoned for the Unitarian point of view. But he was a very conservative Unitarian, and when late in life, on a visit to Italy, he was baptised by a Unitarian minister. He seems to have become less and less Unitarian with advancing years. In the 1832 edition of his *Poems,* the first stanza of his beautiful hymn reads as follows:

Oh, deem not they are blest alone
  Whose lives a peaceful tenor keep;
The Power that pities man has shown
  A blessing for the eyes that weep

In most hymn-books the third line is printed,

> The Anointed Son of God makes known

I had always supposed that this change was made by some orthodox editor; but lately I found a book called *Hymns by William Cullen Bryant,* a presentation copy from the author. And the third line is as one finds it in most hymn-books, so that Bryant must have made the alteration himself, which is decidedly interesting.

The fact that Bryant, in his early years, wrote so much about death, and that his masterpiece, *Thanatopsis,* deals wholly with death both in its title and in its theme, is not in itself a sign of gloom or of religious training or of Puritanism. Nor do I believe that any particular event or the influence of any other poem is responsible for his dwelling so much on thoughts of the tomb. When a young man writes about death, it is not an indication of morbidity, but rather of normalcy. Young poets are usually obsessed by the idea of mortality. Tennyson was a healthy young man; but his first volume is filled with details of dissolution. The reason is sufficiently obvious.

Death appears to youth as a romantic tragedy, and its contrast to their present state is abundantly dramatic; yet in reality it seems far off, and its certainty causes less actual discomfort than a toothache or an unpaid bill. It is easy for youth to contemplate the falling jaw, the glazing eye, and the conquering worm; but when poets are over seventy, they do not dwell on these details with such gusto. At that time Death is not a fancy, but a fact.

Although Bryant was a devout Christian, it is rather surprising that there is nothing Christian, nothing indeed religious, to be found in *Thanatopsis.* It is purely pagan. It is no more Christian than it is American. It might have been written by any poet of any nationality or of any century. We are advised to go to Nature for counsel; she comforts us with the thought of her eternal calm, in contrast to the transitory and feverish existence of man. She teaches us the democracy of death. When we die, we lie down with kings and emperors, with rich and poor; it is a common, a universal experience; we must submit to it with a quiet and a steadfast mind.

It is not, I think, the thought of death, but the love of nature, that has made this poem such a universal favourite. Few poems are more frequently declaimed by school-children, and it would be impossible to set any limits to the extent of its influence. In the year 1908, when I first saw the Grand Canyon of the Colorado, I happened to be talking with the fireman of the locomotive who made several trips daily between Williams and the Canyon. I told him how overwhelmingly impressed I had been, and asked him if daily familiarity made the chasm lose its power. Was it also to him a sublime spectacle, or just an incident in the day's work? "Do you want to know how I feel about it?" said he. And then he repeated the whole of *Thanatopsis!* He had not only learned the poem by heart, but applied its teaching daily in the contemplation of majestic scenery. I suppose some underpaid school-teacher had taught him that poem in his childhood; and this was her reward.

The fruitful influence in Bryant's youth was Wordsworth. He had written *The Embargo* while under the spell of Pope. But between the years 1808 and 1814, he read

Wordsworth, and was born again. This was at a time when comparatively few in New England recognised the genius of the Lake Poet, although nearly all his best work had been written. Once converted, Bryant never faltered. That change from Pope to Wordsworth, indicated on a large scale by the history of English poetry in the nineteenth century, was exemplified individually by Bryant. One of the American's early poems, *A Winter Piece,* opens in a manner quite Wordsworthian:

The time has been that these wild solitudes,
Yet beautiful as wild, were trod by me
Oftener than now; and when the ills of life
Had chafed my spirit—when the unsteady pulse
Beat with strange flutterings—I would wander
forth
And seek the woods. The sunshine on my path
Was to me as a friend. The swelling hills,
The quiet dells retiring far between,
With gentle invitation to explore
Their windings, were a calm society
That talked with me and soothed me.

In the *New York Times,* for 9 January 1899, there is an article wherein the writer endeavours to prove that Bryant was greater than his master. Such a proposition is absurd. *Tintern Abbey,* the great *Ode,* and some of the lyrics, are quite beyond the capacity of the American poet, but the comparison between the two men is interesting and not unproductive of thought.

Bryant's position in American literature is similar to that of Wordsworth in English literature. Bryant wrote about one hundred and sixty poems of which more than one hundred have Nature as a theme. He is our first nature-poet, and in some aspects has never been surpassed by his countrymen. Emerson is more minute, more intimate; but in the large manner, and in the philosophy of peace derived from the contemplation of natural objects, Bryant is as distinctly first with us as Wordsworth is in Britain.

Bryant is the poet of Autumn, as Whittier is of Winter, and Lowell of June. And while Bryant occasionally gives us faithful pictures of autumnal scenery, it is, curiously enough, not the American, but the *English* Autumn that he most characteristically portrays. It would seem almost as if, instead of using his eyes, he had followed literary conventions.

Climate and weather are favourite subjects in poetry; and we should remember that the vast majority of good literature has been written in northern Europe. Suppose there were just as many first-rate poets born in the southern hemisphere as in the northern; then our weather, and our astronomy, and the figures of speech drawn from them would be in continual conflict. Even now, boys and girls studying Shakespeare in Australia and South Africa must find many metaphors that sound strange:

Why wear you such a February face?

Now the American Autumn and the American Winter are quite unlike these seasons in Europe. In America we do not think of a Winter sky as differing from a Summer sky; Winter with us has no lack of sunshine. A typical Winter day in New York or Philadelphia is cold, of course, but has bright Winter sunlight. When we thing of Winter and Summer, we think only of the difference in *temperature.* But in England, France, and Germany, the sky in Autumn and Winter is usually overcast; and there is a sound of abundance of rain. Naturally, therefore, English and Continental poets talk with longing of Italian skies, in contrast to their own; but, as a matter of fact, the Italian sky is not brighter or bluer than the sky over Stamford, Connecticut, or Trenton, New Jersey. English and Continental visitors are always amazed at the brilliance of our Autumn and Winter weather. An English novelist who visited America for the first time told me that during the months of October, November, December in London, she had worked every day by artificial light, because the sky was continually overcast. She arrived in New York about the first of January, accompanied by two umbrellas; she remained here till March; she used her umbrellas only twice. She was astounded at the brightness of our Winter air. America has never received sufficient credit for her Yankee sky; but eventually it will produce its effect on European literature, as it always has on the American temperament. A French professor who came hither to lecture, appeared in New Haven in November; it was a typical American November day, mellow and cloudless, the air soaked in intoxicating sunshine. He could not get over his bewilderment. I asked, "What do you think of our November weather?" He answered, "It is crazy"—*c'est insensé.*

The month of November in America is as different from November in Europe as though it were in a different world. What does Autumn mean in conventional poetry? It signifies gloom, decay, fog, rain, darkness. With us Autumn is all blue and gold, sparkling, radiant, inspiring. I remember in school we children were taught a song, the first line of which was,

"Hail, Autumn, jovial fellow!"

In Europe Autumn at its best is usually pale and dull; just the opposite of our Autumn. And since nearly all the poetry of the world has been written in Europe, European poets have placed their seal on the seasons. They are the weather-vanes of literature.

Now the singular thing is that when Bryant wrote of Autumn he more or less unconsciously imitated the conventional *literary* Autumn, instead of the real one he knew by experience.

"The melancholy days are come, the saddest of the year."

Compare that inaccurate picture with James

Whitcomb Riley's masterpiece. Riley was a poet who had a keen sense of fact. His Autumn was the kind all Americans recognise.

O it's then's the times a feller is a-feelin' at his
best . . .
They's something kind o' hearty-like abcut the
atmosphere
When the heat of summer's over and the coolin'
fall is here—
Of course we miss the flowers, and the blossoms on
the trees,
And the mumble of the hummin'-birds and buzzin'
of the bees;
But the air's so appetizin'; and the landscape
through the haze
Of a crisp and sunny morning of the airly autumn
days
Is a pictur' that no painter has the colorin' to
mock—
When the frost is on the punkin and the fodder's
in the shock.

Even when he writes of June, Bryant managed to infuse into it a tincture of melancholy. June, he thinks, would be a good time for his funeral.

'Twere pleasant, that in flowery June,
When brooks send up a cheerful tune,
And groves a joyful sound,

The sexton's hand, my grave to make,
The soft, green mountain turf should break.

Bryant's pictures of definite objects in nature have been condemned for inaccuracy, but I am inclined to think that in such matters he was usually correct. My own ignorance of flowers prohibits me from taking sides; but there was an editorial in an American newspaper in October 1920, which declared Bryant to be in error concerning the fringed gentian. The writer says, "He has placed it rather late in the season in the second verse of his poem when he wrote:

Thou waitest late and com'st alone
When woods are bare and birds are flown,
And frosts and shortening days portend
The aged year is at an end.

They are seldom severe enough to be noticed when the fringed gentian has finished its blooming, as Burroughs wrote: "The fringed gentian belongs to September and when the severer frosts keep away it runs over into October. But it does not come alone, and the woods are not bare. The closed gentian comes at the same time, and the blue and purple asters are in their glory. Golden rod, turtle-head (chelone), and other fall flowers also abound. When the woods are bare, which does not occur in New England till in or near November, the fringed gentian has long been dead. But it is a small matter that 'Our Poet' has lapsed from grace in such a matter, for has he not given us a beautiful thought to take the place of dry scientific facts?"

A day or two after this article appeared, I received a letter from the Rev. Ralph Herbert White, who informs me that "Bryant's description is quite true for the locality which furnished the material for most of his nature poetry. I lived for seven years in Cummington, the home town of the poet. It is located in the Berkshire highlands, and the Bryant homestead has an altitude of about 2,000 feet. Up there the frosts come very early, frequently during the last of August. The Fringed Gentian comes quite late, and is a rare plant much sought after and loved by the people for the very qualities which Bryant ascribed to it. I have frequently plucked it under just the conditions which he describes."

Bryant resembles Wordsworth in his austerity. He could not let himself go; his poetry lacks warmth of expression. His ode to his sweetheart shows no *desire*. He calls her a "rural maid," and speaks of her calm eyes and the "holy peace" in her breast. I cannot believe that she liked this poem.

But when Bryant leaves human nature alone, and talks of Nature, he is at his best. His poetry of the woods and mountains, plains and seas has the austerity of grandeur. The more impersonal his subject, the better was his treatment of it. The complexity of the human heart was either beyond his capacity, or he was not really interested. Can you imagine Bryant writing a stage-play?

So far as I can make out, Bryant's poetry shows a sonorous bass voice, but not an interesting mind. He had no whimsies. His imagination was under perfect control.

Like Wordsworth, he had no humour. But this limitation did not produce the disasters so regrettable in the Englishman, because Bryant knew he was not funny, and never tried to be. But Wordsworth, like another William, thought he had "a pretty wit."

Bryant was one of the few nineteenth century poets uninfluenced by Byron. There is no trace of the feverish romantic traveller, whose influence on European writers was so powerful, in our American lover of rural life. Nor is there any doubt-struggle in him; no agony of despair; no self-conflict; no seventh chapter of Romans. His battles were all won.

There is something depressing about Bryant's lack of doubt, lack of passion, lack of temptation, lack of conviviality. Let it be granted that water is the best and most healthful of beverages; even so, for poetical purposes, for convivial songs, it lacks inspiration. The following line from Bryant is both anti-climactic and discouraging:

> Fill up the bowl from the brook that glides.

Bryant belongs to Classicism in the best sense of the word. His poems are not paintings—they are statues. He was a great sculptor; he cultivated the lapidary style. He has the purely classical qualities of reserve, restraint, self-suppression, purity of line, objectivity. His literary manner was Greek, his character Roman.

There is little original thought in Bryant. He was meditative rather than thoughtful. He was not pithy, challenging, paradoxical, like Donne or Browning. He does not illuminate a subject, as Goethe invariably did. You cannot imagine him the hero of any such book as the Conversations with Eckermann. His themes are conventional.

Perhaps, for the reasons just stated, his poetic career was not a development. *Thanatopsis* written in his youth, *The Flood of Years* written after he was eighty, are similar in style, movement, and manner. Bryant's career had no beginning, no fruition, no decline. The best work written in his twenties shows no sign of youth, and the latest no sign of age. There is no juvenility in one, and no decay in the other. He is ever the same. The source of the river is as large as its mouth.

When he was an old man, he translated the *Iliad* and the *Odyssey*. In literalness, simplicity, and dignity, his translation is adequate; but Homer had many qualities that were beyond the reach of Bryant. The flexibility of Homer's style is hardly suggested in the English; the multitudinous seas of the Greek poetry, Homer's rippling verse, its charming ease and grace, are not rendered; Bryant's translation is too rigid and monotonous. Perhaps, after all, prose translations are better.

Bryant was once thought to be not only our first poet in time but also in degree; to-day it is clear that two such different men as Poe and Emerson have both surpassed him. Bryant is little read to-day, although a few of his pieces are imperishable. But his place in American literature is secure, for the following reasons: He is the Father of American Poetry: He is preeminently our poet of Nature: He is a master of blank verse: He is a teacher of peace and rest.

There is an elemental quality in his work, that is lacking often in more brilliant writers. His poetry is clear and cold like a mountain lake, and seems to come from an inexhaustible source. There are times when we find him colourless, for he will never satisfy the love of excitement. But in certain moods, when we are weary of doubt and struggle, weary of passion and despair, weary also of cant, affectation, and the straining for paradox—then there is a pleasure in his pathless woods. His calm, cool, silent forests are a refreshing shelter. Some of us, like Hamlet, are too much in the sun; Bryant is a shadowed retreat. When Stedman wished to express exactly what the poetry of Bryant meant to him, he was obliged, as most of us are, to take a phrase from the Bible. Stedman said Bryant was the shadow of a great rock in a weary land.

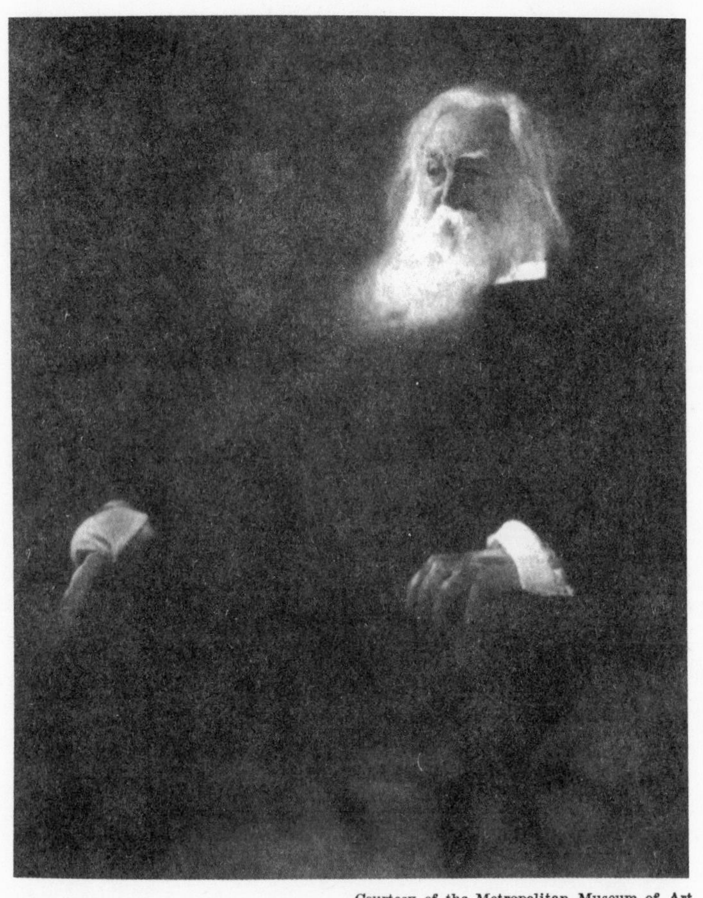

Courtesy of the Metropolitan Museum of Art.

WALT WHITMAN

WHITMAN

Looking over some Whitman manuscripts in the library of Yale University, I found a letter from the poet, which is so characteristic that I place it here at the head of this essay:

Camden, Oct. 14, 1880.

Dear Tom: I got home all safe—We stopped a day & a night at Niagara & had a first rate time—Started the next morning early in an easy comfortable palace car & went on like a streak through New York & Pennsylvania—got into Philadelphia after 11 at night—(we were an hour late)—but the city looked bright & all alive. O I felt as fresh as a lark—I am well, my summer in Canada has done me great good—it is not only the fine country & climate there, but I found such good friends, good quarters, good grub, & every thing that could make a man happy—The last five days I have been down on a jaunt to the sea-shore. . . . I sat hours enjoying it, for it suits me—I was born & brought up near the sea, & I could listen forever to the hoarse music of the surf—Tom I got your paper & handbill, *good for you, boy*—believe me I was pleased to know you won.

Whitman was always cheerful, always the optimist, always the affirmer of life, and the believer in it. He regarded mere animal existence as a huge asset, and conscious living as a continuous joy. He had as little of Mark Twain's pessimism as of his humour; the only point where these representative Americans came in contact was their faith in the universal principle of Democracy.

Who is America's foremost poet? It would be impossible to obtain a majority on a secret ballot for any one. Poe, Emerson, Longfellow, Whittier, Lowell, Whitman have many supporters. Our most popular poet is of course Longfellow; but the greatest? I cannot tell. Emerson and Whitman are the most unconventional, the most free of tradition.

John Burroughs, the faithful disciple of old Walt, divided all poets into two classes—Primary and Secondary. He declared emphatically that Whitman was a greater poet than Tennyson, because Tennyson was a secondary man, and Whitman was primary. He meant that Tennyson followed in broad highways, whereas Whitman blazed a trail. However this may be, I do not believe that Whitman was a greater poet than Tennyson, for the simple reason that his poetry is not so good as Tennyson's.

Yet the reputation of Walt Whitman was never so high as it is now. There were two American centenaries in the year 1919; homage was paid to Lowell and to Whitman. But the latter poet was more widely and more vigorously applauded. There are still many sceptics, many avowed antagonists; but we shall never be rid of him. We cannot say, as some tried to say of a greater poet with the same initials, William Wordsworth,

Here lies W. W.
Who no more will trouble you, trouble you,

for Whitman will trouble us to the end of our lives, and cannot be dismissed with a Podsnappian gesture.

The history of his reputation demands a volume by itself. It began with *Leaves of Grass,* in 1855. That was a notable year in poetry, for it saw also the appearance of Tennyson's *Maud,* Browning's *Men and Women,* Longfellow's *Hiawatha.* *Maud* and

Hiawatha received much ridicule, and *Men and Women* received silence. To-day all these poems are very much alive.

Whitman's admiration of other poets was sufficiently eclectic. His roll-call of the "mighty ones" is as follows: Job, Homer, Æschylus, Dante, Shakespeare, Tennyson, Emerson.

What I shall say about Whitman will please nobody; for I am neither among the worshippers nor the scorners. To me he is neither one-of-the-greatest-poets-of-all-time nor is he a charlatan. I refuse to become excited or polemical in this matter. Whitman needs no defence and attacks cannot hurt him.

It was during the 'seventies that the battle raged most fiercely. To some enthusiasts Whitman was in the front row with Homer and Shakespeare; to other men he was an unclean boor who should be summarily expelled into the outer darkness. Just when the fight was hottest, an obscure young Scot by the name of Robert Louis Stevenson published an essay called *The Gospel According to Walt Whitman* (1878) which in 1923 seems still to be the best appraisal. Let me quote the first paragraph:

Of late years the name of Walt Whitman has been a good deal bandied about in books and magazines. It has become familiar both in good and ill-repute. His works have been largely bespattered with praise by his admirers, and cruelly mauled and mangled by irreverent enemies. Now, whether his poetry is good or bad as poetry, is a matter that may admit of a difference of opinion without alienating those who differ. We could not keep the peace with a man who should put forward claims to taste and yet depreciate the choruses in Samson Agonistes; but I think we may shake hands with one who sees no more in Walt Whitman's volume from a literary point of view, than a farrago of incompetent essays in a wrong direction. That may not be at all our own opinion. We may think that, when a work contains so many unforgetable phrases, it cannot be altogether devoid of literary merit. We may even see passages of a high poetry here and there among its eccentric contents. But when all is said, Walt Whitman is neither a Milton nor a Shakespeare; to appreciate his works is not a condition necessary to salvation; and I would not disinherit a son upon the question, nor even think much the worse of a critic, for I should always have an idea what he meant.

Whitman was born on a farm in Long Island, 31 May 1819. He was the second of nine children, and was called "Walt" to distinguish him from his father Walter. He was the only one of the brood to show any ability. Bliss Perry says the oldest died a lunatic and the youngest was an imbecile.

When he was four years old, the family moved to Brooklyn. Walt had little formal education; at the age of 13, he left school "for good." He did much desultory reading, set type in a printing office, did editorial writing on the *Brooklyn Eagle,* and taught school. This last experience he valued highly. The best thing he got out of his newspaper work was free admission to the New York theatres; he was a constant attendant at plays and operas. Like most men of force and vigour, he loved to read the Bible, and was particularly fond of reading it outdoors, which is one of the severest tests than can be applied to any book. He knocked around the South as a jolly vagabond, doing odd jobs in New Orleans and other places. During the Civil War he did noble and devoted service in taking care of the sick and wounded in the hospitals. He had everlasting patience, reading to the men, and writing letters for them, listening to their talk and telling them stories. In 1873 paralysis seized him. His declining years were spent at Camden, New Jersey. Friends supported him, and he thoroughly enjoyed life, sending copies of his own books to purchasers, composing and revising, receiving daily visits from idolaters and pilgrims who came from everywhere. He became a Sage, and his particular Boswell, Horace Traubel, has left a voluminous and detailed record of his conversations. He died on 26 March 1892.

All of Whitman's unconventionalities, in dress, name, and literary style were deliberately assumed. They were not spontaneous. As a young man, he was something of a macaroni. He dressed in formal and elaborate style, with a frock coat, tall silk hat, and carried a cane. Later he wore a grey flannel shirt, open at the neck, with rolling Byronic collar. In each case he meant to be conspicuous, and succeeded. Originally he signed his work Walter Whitman, and later changed to Walt, as more free-and-easy. His literary career began in an extremely conventional manner; his first publications were in prose, his enemies insist that his later ones were also. When he wrote his first poems, they were written in a correct, conventional, traditional, uninspired metrical form. Probably no famous writer ever made more revolutionary changes in his mental attitude towards life and art.

At the age of twenty-three, Whitman made his first appearance as an author. In a periodical called *The New World,* New York, November 1842, there appeared what was described as an "original temperance novel,"

FRANKLIN EVANS: OR, THE INEBRIATE
A Tale of the Times by
WALTER WHITMAN

This is written in an insufferable style, stilted, sophomoric, melodramatic, sentimental, turgid, impossible. It sounds like a burlesque on a temperance tract, but it was serious. T. S. Arthur's *Ten Nights in a Barroom,* a hot favourite with children, is mild and restrained in comparison with *Franklin Evans: The Inebriate.*

In 1850, in a miscellany called *Voices from the Press,* appeared a short story by Whitman, with the fantastic title, *The Tomb Blossoms.* Here the country is praised in contrast to the city, a strange point of view when we remember *Crossing Brooklyn Ferry.* The style of this tale is no better than that of its predecessor.

Meanwhile, Whitman was studying verse-forms and casting about for something by which to attract the attention of the public. For whether he was a genius or a faker, one thing is certain. Never was there a man who so loved publicity. The lime-light was as necessary to his personal comfort as water is to a fish. He could not endure obscurity.

Bliss Perry, in his *Life of Whitman,* has pointed out the remarkable similarity between a free-verse poem, *The Lily and the Bee,* by Samuel Warren, published in 1851, and the style of *Leaves of Grass,* 1855. It is impossible to avoid the conclusion, that although Whitman did not borrow from Warren, he had read him with profit. The rhythmic prose of the Bible and the rhapsodical pages of Ossian had been familiar to Whitman since childhood. Evidently he feared that *Leaves of Grass* might be called an imitation of Ossian, for in the notes that he wrote for his own guidance, we find "Don't fall into the Ossianic *by any chance.*"

When *Leaves of Grass* appeared in 1855, Whitman hoped that it would make a sensation—that it would either be greeted as the work of a new and authentic prophet, or that it would become a public scandal. To his dismay, it fell flat, and attracted hardly any attention. He therefore wrote long and laudatory reviews of it, which appeared anonymously in various periodicals. But even these puffs failed to start a fire.

Whitman sent out presentation copies to distinguished men, and in one instance the result was magnificent. On 21 July 1855, Emerson wrote a glowing and generous letter, that filled the new poet with natural and justifiable exultation. Here are some of the phrases in which Emerson expressed his recognition and tribute. "I find it the most extraordinary piece of wit and wisdom that America has yet contributed. I am very happy in reading it, as great power makes us happy. . . . I find incomparable things, said incomparably well, as they must be. . . . I greet you at the beginning of a great career." This last phrase, Whitman, without asking permission, placed in letters of gold, signed R. W. Emerson, on the outside of the cover of the new edition in 1856, which gave the philosopher the severest test of his tranquillity that he had ever been forced to meet.

Many short reviews of the book consigned it to the garbage-heap, and some insisted that the author should be arrested. Thus there began that fierce quarrel about *Leaves of Grass* that will never be completely and finally settled. The reason is simple enough; there are poems of amazing originality and beauty, and there are passages which never should have been printed. Whitman was a man of genius; but he had no humour, no taste, and no sense of proportion. On this whole question young Mr. Stevenson, in 1878, said the last word:

In his desire to accept all facts, facts loyally and simply, it fell within his programme to speak at some length and with some plainness on what is, for I really do not know what reason, the most delicate of subjects. Seeing in that one of the most serious and interesting parts of life, he was aggrieved that it should be looked upon as ridiculous or shameful. No one speaks of maternity with his tongue in his cheek; and Whitman made a bold push to set the sanctity of fatherhood beside the sanctity of motherhood, and introduce this also among the things that can be spoken of without a blush or a wink. But the Philistines have been too strong; and, to say truth, Whitman has rather played the fool. We may be thoroughly conscious that his end is improving; that it would be a good thing if a window were opened on these close privacies of life; that on this subject, as on all others, he now and then lets fall a pregnant saying. But we are not satisfied. We feel that he was not the man for so difficult an enterprise. He loses our sympathy in the character of a poet by attracting too much of our attention in that of a Bull in a China Shop. And where, by a little more art, we might have been solemnized ourselves, it is too often Whitman himself alone who is solemn in the face of an audience somewhat indecorously amused.

In dismissing this subject, there is no doubt that Whitman was sincere. But there is also no doubt that his chronic itch for publicity made him more daring than would otherwise have been the case. Since we know how intensely he loved to attract attention, that the chief delight in his life was to be talked about, it is as certain as anything can be that he deliberately put in passages which he believed would make a sensation. They certainly eventually helped to sell his book; they help to sell it now. Emerson pleaded with him in vain; Whitman insisted that nothing should be struck out, and that no abridged version of his poems should appear. Shortly before his death, he finally consented to the publication of a volume of *Selected Poems,* chosen with great skill by Arthur Stedman, who said in his preface, "This edition of Mr. Whitman's poems is, on his part, a concession to friendship. He has not abandoned his position, but has yielded to urgent request." Mr. Stedman did the old poet a valuable service. Those who had heard of Whitman only as a charlatan or as an immoral writer, found in this little volume of Selections enough authentic poetry to change their attitude.

It was not long before parodies appeared, for the subject invited that form of criticism which can best be expressed in parody and burlesque. Whoever is interested in this branch of Whitmania, may now be referred to a book published in 1923, called *Parodies on Walt Whitman,* edited by Henry S. Saunders, with a disarming preface by Christopher Morley. The parodies begin with the year 1857, and close with 1921. Most of them do not seem nearly so funny to us as they must have seemed to their authors. The times have changed, and Whitman is an accepted poet. His peculiarities are so well known that the parody now fails of its intended effect. The best one in the book, as might be expected, is that by the late H. C. Bunner.

The reason why, with a few exceptions like Emerson, *Leaves of Grass* was received either with silence or with abuse, was because of its unlikeness to conventional poetry. When genius supplies a demand, as in the instances of Byron and Tennyson, immediate popularity is the result. There has always been, there is now, and there always will be, a sharp demand for beautifully melodious poetry. But where Genius has to create the demand as well as the supply, where the new forms or the new treatment are entirely unlike what the world is looking for, then the way towards recognition is difficult. Original genius is outside of the law of supply and demand. There was no demand for Browning, or for Ibsen, or for Wagner, or for Whitman; these four men had to create the demand as well as the supply. The mass of people are conventional, like schoolboys, and they distrust and often hate anything that is unconventional or even unusual. What first impressed the public in the works of these Four was not its greatness, but its *strangeness;* that quality of strangeness had to overcome the natural opposition and inertia of humanity, before the greatness could be recognised. For the conventional public opinion, as expressed in print hundreds of times on these four men, was, that whatever they might be, they were assuredly not what they professed to be. Ibsen was not a dramatist; Wagner was not a musician; Browning and Whitman were not poets.

How fortunate it was for these four that they all lived to be old! Had they died in middle life, they would have died unrecognised. But Wagner, Ibsen, Browning, and Whitman received in old age the tribute of universal fame, which must have been all the sweeter for having been long deferred.

Yet although Whitman died a famous poet, his reputation then was nothing to what it is now. In the 'nineties, the controlling voice in English poetry was Rudyard Kipling, who was as unlike Whitman as could be imagined. Kipling had vitality, originality, and force; but he expressed himself carefully in conventional metres. The whole tendency of verse in both England and in America then seemed towards more rather than less restraint in form; the most popular poet in America, James Whitcomb Riley, was conventional metrically. He despised Whitman and all his works. Furthermore, although Whitman's admirers insisted that he was the voice of democracy, the common people never heard him gladly. The average Americans read Longfellow and Whittier, because those poets best expressed their own inarticulate feelings; they knew little about Whitman and cared less. He, the poet of democracy, was read chiefly by a few literary aristocrats in Europe and in America, whose jaded taste required something new.

But owing to the renaissance of poetry which began in Europe and in America a few years before the Great War, and was definitely stimulated by that catastrophe, the general public began to read Whitman, and for the first time, he became a popular poet. Again, a renaissance of poetry necessarily means experimentation; and during the last ten years many young poets are avowed followers of Whitman, both in writing free verse, and in their fondness for new forms of expression In a word, Whitman has come into his own.

It is perhaps natural that in the nineteenth century Whitman had more admirers in Europe than in America. He was regarded as the poet of Democracy, America's authentic voice. We, who lived in the atmosphere and environment which he tried to express, would not naturally have been so impressed as those dwelling afar off. Europeans have always been trying to find some one who should reveal the American spirit, and many thought the search was rewarded in *Leaves of Grass.*

When discussion of Whitman became common in England, there arose the same violent difference of opinion as was evident here. Dante Rossetti, in a letter to William Allingham, in April 1856, wrote, "I have not been so happy in loathing anything for a long while—except, I think, *Leaves of Grass,* by that Orson of yours. I should like just to have the writing of a valentine to him in one of the reviews." Later, in 1878, in commenting on his brother's *Lives of Famous Poets,* Dante Rossetti said: "I am sorry to see that name winding up a summary of great poets." The two brothers never agreed about this, for in 1869, William Michael Rossetti wrote, "That glorious man Whitman will one day be known as one of the greatest sons of Earth, a few steps below Shakespeare on the throne of immortality." Swinburne's opinion about Whitman suffered a curious change. When he first read *Leaves of Grass,* shortly after its appearance, he was enthusiastic and spoke highly of it. Even as late as 1885 he wrote, "I retain a very cordial admiration for not a little of Whitman's earlier work." But in 1887 Swinburne made a thorough recantation, saying that Whitman's Muse was a "drunken apple-woman, indecently sprawling in the slush and garbage of the gutter amid the rotten refuse of her overturned fruit-stall."

In America, Dartmouth College can claim the honour of being the first academic institution to treat Whitman officially with respect. He was invited to deliver the Commencement Poem in 1872, and he accepted, writing and reading on that occasion a poem originally called *As a Strong Bird on Pinions Free.* In the *Complete Works* this title was changed to *Thou Mother with Thy Equal Brood.* In the same year of its delivery he published the Dartmouth poem, with a preface so important, and made even more so by the years 1914-1918, that it is necessary to quote from it.

The impetus and ideas urging me, for some years past, to an utterance, or attempt at utterance, of New World songs, and an epic of Democracy, having already had their publish'd expression, as well as I can expect to give it, in "Leaves of Grass," the present and any future pieces from me are really but the surplusage forming after that volume, or the wake eddying behind it. I fulfill'd in that an imperious conviction, and the commands of my nature as total and irresistible as those which make the sea flow, or the globe revolve. But of this supplementary volume, I confess I am not so certain. Having from early manhood abandon'd the business pursuits and applications usual in my time and country, and obediently yielded myself up ever since to the impetus mention'd, and to the work of expressing those ideas, it may be that mere habit has got dominion of me, when there is no real need of saying anything further. But what is life but an experiment? and mortality but an exercise? with reference to results beyond. And so shall my poems be. If incomplete here, and superfluous there, *n'importe*—the earnest trial and persistent exploration shall at least be mine, and other success failing shall be success enough. I have been more anxious, anyhow, to suggest the songs of vital endeavour and manly evolution, and furnish something for races of outdoor athletes, than to make perfect rhymes, or reign in the parlours. I ventur'd from the beginning my own way, taking chances—and would keep on venturing.

I will therefore not conceal from any persons,

known or unknown to me, who take an interest in the matter, that I have the ambition of devoting yet a few years to poetic composition. The mighty present age! To absorb and express in poetry, anything of it—of its world—America—cities and States—the years, the events of our Nineteenth century—the rapidity of movement—the violent contrasts, fluctuations of light and shade, of hope and fear—the entire revolution made by science in the poetic method—these great new underlying facts and new ideas rushing and spreading everywhere;—truly a mighty age! As if in some colossal drama, acted again like those of old under the open sun, the Nations of our time, and all the characteristics of Civilization, seem hurrying, stalking across, flitting from wing to wing, gathering, closing up, towards some long-prepared, most tremendous denouement. Not to conclude the infinite scenes of the race's life and toil and happiness and sorrow, but haply that the boards be cleared from oldest, worst incumbrances, accumulations, and Man resume the eternal play anew, and under happier, freer auspices. To me, the United States are important because in this colossal drama they are unquestionably designated for the leading parts, for many a century to come. In them history and humanity seem to seek to culminate. Our broad areas are even now the busy theatre of plots, passions, interests, and suspended problems, compared to which the intrigues of the past of Europe, the wars of dynasties, the scope of kings and kingdoms, and even the development of peoples, as hitherto, exhibit scales of measurement comparatively narrow and trivial. And on these areas of ours, as on a stage, sooner or later, something like an *eclaircissement* of all the past civilization of Europe and Asia is probably to be evolved.

The leading parts. Not to be acted, emulated here, by us again, that rôle till now foremost in history—not to become a conqueror nation, or to achieve the glory of mere military, or diplomatic, or commercial superiority—but to become the grand producing land of nobler men and women—of copious races, cheerful, healthy, tolerant, free—to become the most friendly nation (the United States indeed)—the modern composite nation, form'd from all, with room for all, welcoming all immigrants—accepting the work of our own interior development, as the work fitly filling ages and ages to come;—the leading nation of peace, but neither ignorant nor incapable of being the leading nation of war;—not the man's nation only, but the woman's nation—a land of splendid mothers, daughters, sisters, wives. . . .

The Four Years' War is over—and in the peaceful, strong, exciting, fresh occasions of to-day, and of the future, that strange, sad war is hurrying even now to be forgotten. The camp, the drill, the lines of sentries, the prisons, the hospitals—(ah! the hospitals!)—all have passed away—all seem now like a dream. A new race, a young and lusty generation, already sweeps in with oceanic currents, obliterating the war, and all its scars, its mounded graves, and all its reminiscences of hatred, conflict, death. So let it be obliterated. I say the life of the present and the future makes undeniable demands upon us each and all, south, north, east, west. To help put the United States (even if only in imagination) hand in hand, in one unbroken circle in a chant—to rouse them to the unprecedented grandeur of the part they are to play, and are even now playing—to the thought of their great future, and the attitude conform'd to it—especially their great esthetic, moral, scientific future (of which their vulgar material and political present is but as the preparatory tuning of instruments by an orchestra), these, as hitherto, are still, for me, among my hopes, ambitions.

How far and in what sense is Whitman an original writer? It is often stated that he is one of our most original thinkers and poets. His leading ideas are not original. He expresses chiefly enthusiasm for humanity, love of the race, the worship of democracy; all this is emphatically and at times impressively uttered. But it can be found in Rousseau, and has been more poetically expressed by Shelley. Has then Whitman nothing new or important to tell us? He says "Rejoice in yourselves: in life: in all your bodily functions." Had he proclaimed this some centuries earlier, he might have been called original. The revolt against asceticism, the refusal to regard the human body as vile, the unwillingness to consider human life on earth as a mere vestibule to eternity—these are fundamental ideas in Whitman. But he was by no means the first to proclaim them.

I should say that Whitman was more unconventional than original. As he discarded fashionable clothing, so he discarded fashionable opinions. In America he was more "different" than he would have seemed in Europe. Here he was against the Puritan tradition, against what was understood and agreed upon as decency, against small-town mentality, against any and all reserve. His manners shocked Americans as they could not have shocked Europeans; for example, he was forever kissing men, which simply "isn't done" in America. I remember when a European pianist played in Boston, he was entertained after the concert by an exclusive club. He caused a sensation by insisting on kissing every one of the men who were presented to him. It took them a long while to recover.

Much of the shock caused by Whitman's poetry really had more to do with literary etiquette than with thought. It was largely a question of manners. Now the older a civilisation is, the freer and franker the behaviour and conversation of the people. In the nineteenth century, things were discussed in books and at dinner-tables on the Continent which were never mentioned in America. And what is true of an old country as compared with a new is true of a large city as compared with a village. Country bumpkins will snigger secretly over vulgarities; but village society says limb when it means leg; prefers circumlocutions to direct statements; and still prefers rhetorical oratory to simple plain language. It is the last citadel of the old-fashioned spell-binder.

In the same way, old countries are more tolerant of religious and political heresies than new ones; and in any country, there is more freedom of speech in a big city than in a village. During and after the Great War, there was more individual freedom of speech in England than in America; and in America, there was more freedom in New York than anywhere else, much more than in country villages. Many were surprised that the penalties—twenty years in prison, for example—

that were given to persons who expressed heretical political opinions in America were unknown in England; this is really natural, and is simply a register of intellectual levels. We had and have the small-town view, that cannot comprehend opinions contrary to those current in the village.

Whitman's lack of reserve on all topics and his unconventionalities were startling in America in 1855.

In one respect he had the wisdom of the great poets. He was never an opportunist; he did not deal with "timely" questions. Though intensely American, as a poet he was universal and dealt with universal and unchangeable things like human passions and the stars. He was a revolutionist in art, but he was never a political revolutionist; he was not a socialist, not an anarchist, not a political reformer. He was kept from all this not only by his intense individualism, which would have made it impossible for him to cooperate with any organisation, but by a kind of instinctive wisdom, which made him deal with fundamental and eternal things, the true subjects of art.

Whitman's religion was certainly not

Christianity, except in one important aspect, his belief in the brotherhood of man. Not only was he devoid even of a grain of Christian faith, he was definitely in opposition to Christian teaching. If I understand Christianity at all, it is opposed to human instincts; it proposes to substitute unselfishness for selfishness, modesty for greed, purity for sensuality, giving for taking, self-control for self-assertion. The reason why Christianity is so unpopular at the present moment—for unpopular it certainly is—is not because it is opposed to reason, for it is in harmony with the only reasonable way of life. It is unpopular because it places a constant veto on human instincts, and we are living (1923) in a post-war relaxation and hatred of all restraint. Possibly one reason why Christianity has never been popular in any period with the younger generation is because early in life instinct is stronger than reason; wisdom comes, if at all, by experience. Christianity is of course a positive, not a negative religion; it is a religion to live by, not to die by; but, as Browning said, it teaches original sin, the corruption of man's heart. Christianity never uses palliatives or surface remedies; it calls for regeneration, for a new birth, for a complete change in emphasis.

Keats said in one of his letters, "O for a life of sensations rather than of thoughts!" Whitman is more of a sensationalist than a thinker. The tentacles of his mind were all feelers; he was like an Æolian harp, to be played upon by the chance winds of heaven. To regard him as a profound philosopher, prophet, or great teacher is idle; he shows us how to enjoy life, how to appreciate beauty, how to become ever more sensitive to impressions, but he very seldom stimulates the mind. Professor Henry A. Beers is very near the final truth about him, when he says, "If a large, good-natured, clean, healthy animal could write poetry, it would write such poetry as the *Leaves of Grass.* It would tell how good it is to lie and bask in the warm sun; to stand in cool, flowing water, to be naked in the fresh air; to troop with friendly companions and embrace one's mate."

One of the reasons why Whitman is so popular at this moment is because many of our novelists and men of letters have substituted the animal for the spiritual attitude towards life. We used to be told that we should conquer the beast in us; now we are told every day to imitate the animals, to be like them, do what we please, and never on any account be sorry afterwards. There are many prominent writers to-day to whom the word sin is obsolete. They are, consciously or unconsciously, followers of Whitman. I cannot imagine old Walt suffering from anything like remorse.

So far as he had a religion, it can be described by the well-known phrase, "cosmic emotion," concerning which Professor W. K. Clifford wrote an interesting essay. Man must have some religion or some substitute for religion; I do not believe the average human being can live without it. If all theistic belief is dead, the religion of nature remains. One goes out at night, contemplates the stars, and feels oneself a part of the universe. To Whitman this was always a solemnising thought. "The huge and thoughtful night." He was sincere in what religion he had. When a dying soldier asked Whitman to read him a chapter in the New Testament, he read the account of the crucifixion. "The poor, wasted young man ask'd me to read the following chapter also, how Christ rose again. I read very slowly, for Oscar was feeble. It pleased him very much, yet the tears were in his eyes. He ask'd me if I enjoyed religion. I said, 'Perhaps not, my dear, in the way you mean, and yet, may-be, it is the same thing.' He said, 'It is my chief reliance.' He talk'd of death, and said he did not fear it."

Whitman was a careful student of rhythm, and had read the Bible to advantage. His best lines have superb rolling music that needs no rime, although he did not disdain rime. His most famous poem is also the most conventional in metre, "Oh Captain! my Captain." Whitman became tired of hearing this praised, both because he did not wish to be regarded as a man of one poem, and because it was so unlike his more characteristic work. When some one praised it one day, he exclaimed angrily, "Oh, *damn* My Captain!" His impatience is easy to understand. We are told that a man voted against Aristides because he was tired of hearing him called The Just, but think how utterly weary Aristides himself must have been.

I hold no brief for free verse; other things being equal, I prefer regular metrical forms. But there are certain subjects, which, if Whitman had described them in sonnets, could not have been so impressively brought to our perceptions as Whitman brings them with his irregularities. Take the lines he wrote in Platte Cañon, Colorado.

Spirit that form'd this scene,
These tumbled rock-piles grim and red,
These reckless heaven-ambitious peaks,
These gorges, turbulent-clear streams, this naked freshness,
These formless wild arrays, for reasons of their own,
I know thee, savage spirit—we have communed together,
Mine too such wild arrays, for reasons of their own;
Was't charged against my chants they had forgotten art?
To fuse within themselves its rules precise and delicatesse?
The lyrist's measur'd beat, the wrought-out temple's grace—column and polish'd arch forgot?
But thou that revelest here—spirit that form'd this scene,
They have remembered thee.

Although Whitman has an unassailable place in literature, and although he has profoundly influenced many young poets, and at no time more than now, his own method—free verse—has not yet given birth to anything supreme. The best free-verse writing in the English language is still to be found in Whitman, and not in the works of his imitators or followers. They have done well, but not supremely well; and their best is below the best conventional work done by their contemporaries. Whitman was undoubtedly a great poet; but who are the leading English poets of the twentieth century? Kipling, Thompson, Phillips, Housman, Henley, Hardy, Hodgson, De La Mare, Noyes, Masefield, Watson, Brooke, Flecker, Davies; and in America, our three leading living poets are Robinson, Lindsay, and Frost. Neither in England nor in America are the leaders distinguished for free verse composition, but rather for the opposite. Therefore the old battle-cry, that Whitman's is "the poetry of the future," seems particularly untrue.

There are still those who would deny Whitman the rank of great poet. But we should remember that the Republic of Letters is not a social club; genius cannot be blackballed, and Whitman was a man of genius. He often expressed a universal idea in a permanently beautiful phrase. His greatness, indeed, consists not so much in whole poems as in phrases. He had a particular talent for first lines and titles, so that the Table of Contents or Index of First Lines to Whitman's Complete Poems would seem full of promise to one who should stumble on the book without previous knowledge. Like some grocers, he put the best apples on top. Looking down the *Table of Contents,* one feels that the Table itself is a Poem.

In Cabin'd Ships at Sea
I Hear America Singing
Shut not Your Doors to Me, Proud Libraries
Out of the Rolling Ocean the Crowd
Once I Pass'd Through a Populous City
I Heard You Solemn-Sweet Pipes of the Organ
When I Heard at the Close of the Day
I Saw in Louisiana a Live-Oak Growing
This Moment Yearning and Thoughtful
Fast-Anchored Eternal O Love
O You Whom I Often and Silently Come
Song of the Open Road
Song of the Redwood Tree
Song of the Rolling Earth
Youth, Day, Old Age, and Night
Pioneers! O Pioneers!
Out of the Cradle Endlessly Rocking
As I Ebb'd With the Ocean of Life

Whitman

To the Man-of-War Bird
The World Below the Brine
On the Beach at Night Alone
Song for All Seas, All Ships
When I Heard the Learn'd Astronomer
The Dalliance of the Eagles
Beat! Beat! Drums!
From Paumanok Starting I Fly Like a Bird
Song of the Banner at Daybreak
Rise O Days from Your Fathomless Deeps
Cavalry Crossing a Ford
By the Bivouac's Fitful Flame
Vigil Strange I Kept on the Field One Night
A Sight in Camp in the Daybreak Gray and Dim
As Toilsome I Wander'd Virginia's Woods
Year that Trembled and Reel'd Beneath Me.
Give Me the Splendid Silent Sun
Over the Carnage Rose Prophetic a Voice
I Saw Old General at Bay
Ethiopia Saluting the Colors
O Tan-Faced Prairie-Boy
Look Down Fair Moon
When Lilacs Last in the Dooryard Bloom'd
O Captain, My Captain
Hush'd be the Camps To-day
By Blue Ontario's Shore
There was a Child Went Forth
The Singer in the Prison
Warble for Lilac-Time
O Star of France
An Old Man's Thought of School
Proud Music of the Storm

Prayer of Columbus
Darest Thou Now O Soul
Yet, Yet, Ye Downcast Hours
As if a Phantom Caress'd Me
That Music Always Round Me
A Noiseless Patient Spider
Thou Mother with Thy Equal Brood
Thou Orb Aloft Full-Dazzling
The Mystic Trumpeter
To a Locomotive in Winter
Ah Poverties, Wincings, and Sulky Retreats
Weave in, My Hardy Life
By Broad Potomac's Shore
From Far Dakota's Cañons
Spirit That Form'd this Scene
As I Walk These Broad Majestic Days
The Sobbing of the Bells
Joy, Shipmate, Joy
Sands at Seventy
Good-By, My Fancy

The art of poetry is an art of expression; we are all poets at heart. We all have imagination and poetic thought, else why should we find in the great poets so clear an echo of ourselves? The more distinct the echo, the greater the poet. But we are inarticulate; we cannot express ourselves; we love music, and we cannot sing. The great poets are the spokesmen for humanity. Whitman spoke out for us all. There are passages in such poems as *Columbus, When Lilacs Last, The Man-of-War Bird,* that rhythmically sing thoughts that are universal.

Furthermore, there is something healthy in his optimism. He was never petulant, never cynical, never despairing. To him Life was good. He belongs not among those who have despised the supreme gift of life, not among the deniers, but among the Affirmers. He was entirely free from the prevailing modern disease, the fear of life. He loved life, and welcomed experience; he was devoid of fear. He calls upon us to rejoice; to use our eyes and our senses; to commune in rapture with the sea and the stars.

In a certain sense, Whitman interpreted America to Europe; and to America he tried to interpret the universe.

THOREAU

America never produced a more original writer than Henry David Thoreau. In the days of his earthly pilgrimage he was regarded by his enemies with contemptuous hostility and by his friends with amused tolerance. Only a few had any conception of the true greatness of the man, and even fewer prophesied the permanence of his fame. To-day, sixty years after his death, two things are clear; first, the essential nobility of his character; second, the steady advance of his literary reputation. He was not either a dangerous or a harmless crank, because he was not a crank at all; he was an original philosopher, who had observed much and meditated deeply, and whose actions were the fruit of silent hours. As a writer, he is not the equal of Emerson or Hawthorne, but he is certain to outlive many of his more showy contem-

From the Rowse Crayon in the Public Library at Concord, Mass.
Reproduced by permission of Houghton Mifflin Company.

HENRY DAVID THOREAU
In 1854

poraries. There is perhaps no one whose "place" in the future seems more absolutely assured than that of Thoreau. His literary work was as honest as his mechanical; its foundations were solid, and the structure weather-defying. As some men grow strong by contact with harsh winds and severe frost, so the chill of Time, which subdues so many flourishing fames, seems only to ripen and harden and strengthen the reputation of Thoreau.

At his birth, 17 July 1817, his parents gave him three names in alphabetical order; David Henry Thoreau. But he was called Henry, and later he rearranged his name, just as he rearranged his life, to suit himself. He was born in Concord, Massachusetts, and thus belongs to the famous Concord School not by adoption, as was the case with Hawthorne, but by right of birth. His grandfather Thoreau came from the Isle of Jersey in the English Channel; his father and mother were the "right sort" for such a child, as they loved Nature, and in the education of their children placed the things of the spirit first. Edward Emerson, in his little book on Thoreau, which should be read by every student of the naturalist, says, "A near neighbour and friend told me that for years the family had on ordinary days neither tea, coffee, sugar, nor other luxuries, that the girls might have the piano which their early musical taste showed they would want, and the education of all, especially the sending of the younger son to college, might be provided for; and yet her table was always attractive, and the food abundant and appetizing. There were two daughters and two sons, of whom Henry was the younger."

The health of children should naturally be to their parents an object of solicitude; now that Hygiene is in many households the only God worshipped, there is little to fear on the score of bodily neglect. Many mothers seem to believe that if their childrens' bodies are clean and healthy, nothing further will be required. Others insist on the addition of good manners. But is there to-day that fierce passion for the minds and souls of boys and girls that used to characterise New England parents? There is no doubt in my mind, although I am not a Catholic, that Catholic parents are more particular about the religious training of their children than the average

Protestant. Furthermore, why are children allowed to go to the motion pictures four or five times a week, observe with almost professional acumen the musical-comedies, read only ephemeral sensations, and talk only about mechanical devices such as radios and the various styles of automobiles? In many instances not only do the children regulate their lives according to their own sweet will, but they regulate both the activities and the opinions of their parents. The sole reason why many middle-aged men took an active part in the recent war, where often they were only in the way of others, was because they were afraid of future questions by their children. "What did you do in the Great War?" Surely there ought to be some better reason for conduct than fear of youthful opinion. In many cases not only have parents given up religious training for their children, but have given up religion for themselves, in order to be in harmony with the indolent and undisciplined minds of their offspring. I have repeatedly observed this interesting and stultifying mode of behaviour.

Not long ago I read in the *New York Tribune* an interview with Arthur Bodansky, the conductor of the Metropolitan Opera House Orchestra. He was asked for his opinions on various tendencies of the day, and he said that his children were never allowed to hear jazz, but only first-rate music; that they were not allowed to read trash, but only good books, etc., etc. How strange, how obsolete such language sounded! And how many parents, reading that interview, must have winced at the word "allowed," and wondered how in the world Mr. Bodansky contrived to have any restraining influence whatever on his children!

Thoreau's father and mother knew the woods and fields around Concord as they knew the interior of their own house, and it was in their company that Henry first learned to understand and love animal and plant life. His mother was what we used to call in New England a "capable" woman; she managed the house, her husband, and her children. She was a half-head taller than her consort and would have been prominent in any company, owing to her love of display, her bold, adventurous spirit, and her amazing flow of talk. She loved bright colours and flaunting ribbons, and was not afraid to wear them anywhere and always. When she was seventy years old, she called on the aunt of Ralph Waldo Emerson, who was eighty-four. During the conversation, Miss Emerson kept her eyes closed, and at the end, she remarked, with that delightful candour that used to characterise Concord folks, "Perhaps you noticed, Mrs. Thoreau, that I closed my eyes during your call. I did so because I did not wish to look on the ribbons you are wearing, so unsuitable for a child of God and a person of your years."

The father, John Thoreau, was quiet, unassertive, and deaf; the defect was perhaps not altogether a misfortune, for his wife was so voluble that Sanborn, the biographer, says "She fully verified the Oriental Legend, which accounts for the greater loquacity of women by the fact that nine baskets of talk were let down from heaven to Adam and Eve in their garden, and that Eve glided forward first and secured six of them." Nearly all the stories of the fluency of women have been written by men. For my own part, I do not think that women have any monopoly of verbosity. It is an individual, rather than a sex trait. I have known men who could talk for hours with no more fatigue and no more variety than a dog barking in the night.

It would be an error to suppose that Cynthia Thoreau was a disagreeable woman. Her husband and children lived with her happily, even merrily.

The nearest approach to literature reached by any member of the family until Henry began to write, was the manufacture of lead-pencils, the bread-winning occupation of the father. He made the best pencils to be found anywhere, and Henry gave such attention, thought and experiments to the enterprise that immense improvements were made, which made the business remunerative. Henry had extraordinary mechanical skill, and was an admirable worker with all sorts of tools, an excellent surveyor, gardener, and farmer; and if he had not determined to live the life of the mind, could have made a satisfactory income in any one of a variety of occupations. He was that rare person, "a handy man about the house," and was forever fixing up his own and his neighbours' fences, stoves, windows, and roofs. I look with despair on that kind of skill, being totally without it. If anything is wrong with my bicycle, watch or window-sash, I immediately consult a specialist. I know no more about such things than I know of my own insides. If I were cast on a desert island, I should be helpless; whereas Thoreau would have immediately risen to leadership like the Admirable Crichton.

Thoreau went to Harvard and was graduated with the class of 1837. An extreme individualist, it was natural that he did not value college life and training very highly. He had prepared himself admirably at Concord in classics and mathematics; his knowledge of Greek literature was unusually good, and that best of all foundations for true culture is evident in his literary work. He won a scholarship, which partly defrayed his expenses; he taught school during vacations, earned money in various ways; and he lived with an economy in expenditure which would today seem miraculous. He never made the slightest attempt to impress either his instructors or his classmates, and both Faculty and undergraduates naturally thought little of him. In return, he was quite content to let any and all of them think of him exactly what they liked.

During the college years, his chief extra-curriculum activity was the Library. He said afterwards it was the best thing Harvard had to offer. There he read extensively in ancient and modern literature, which he turned to good account later. The year after graduation, wishing to teach school, he obtained the following recommendation from a man whose good opinion was decidedly worth having.

> I cordially recommend Mr. Henry D. Thoreau, a graduate of Harvard University in August, 1837, to the confidence of such parents or guardians as may propose to employ him as an instructor. I have the highest confidence in Mr. Thoreau's moral character, and in his intellectual ability. He is an excellent scholar, a man of energy and kindness, and I shall esteem the town fortunate that secures his services.
>
> RALPH WALDO EMERSON.
>
> Concord, May 2, 1838.

The Senior Pastor of the First Church in Concord, Dr. Ezra Ripley, wrote in the same week a recommendation which contained the following sentence: "His scholarship and moral character will bear the strictest scrutiny."

College graduates with observing eyes

know that men's characters do not change very much after graduation; they develop, but as a rule they do not change. It is highly symptomatic, that Thoreau, who was graduated at the age of twenty, in his Commencement oration, held up the ideal of the Individualist. Here are some extracts from his address given by Edward Emerson.

> Let men, true to their natures, cultivate the moral affections, lead manly and independent lives. . . . The sea will not stagnate, the earth will be as green as ever, and the air as pure. This curious world which we inhabit is more wonderful than it is convenient; more beautiful than it is useful; it is more to be admired and enjoyed than used. The order of things should be somewhat reversed; the seventh should be man's day of toil, wherein to earn his living by the sweat of his brow; and the other six his Sabbath of the affections and the soul,—in which to range this widespread garden, and drink in the soft influences and sublime revelations of Nature.

Henry and his brother John opened a school in Concord, which was directed on independent lines, but where the pupils were faithfully taught. John died in the full tide of young manhood of a slight cut which caused lockjaw. This was an unspeakable sorrow to Henry, as no two brothers were ever closer in affection. For some years Henry worked in the pencil factory, was private tutor on Staten Island—what an ideal private teacher!—was a land surveyor, and carpenter. Was there ever a more characteristic remark than his on nail-driving? "I would not be one of those who will foolishly drive a nail into mere lath and plastering; such a deed would keep me awake nights. Give me a hammer and let me feel for the furring. Drive a nail home, and clinch it so faithfully, that you can wake up in the night and think of your work with satisfaction, a work at which you would not be ashamed to invoke the Muse. So will help you God, and so only. Every nail driven should be as another rivet in the machine of the universe, you carrying on the work."

It was in August 1839, that the two brothers made their famous week-journey on the Concord and Merrimack rivers, the subject of Henry's first book. From 1841 to 1843 he lived in Emerson's household in Concord, being exactly the kind of pupil that every great teacher loves to have. He was inspired by his master, but never imitated him. From

1845 to 1847 he lived in his hut at Walden Pond. He died of tuberculosis on 6 May 1862. He was buried in Concord cemetery, where he lies with his peers, Emerson and Hawthorne, all three men of literary genius and independent minds.

When he was dying, his aunt asked him, "Henry, have you made your peace with God?" He whispered, "I did not know we had ever quarrelled."

The chief element in his character was Independence. He must live his own life, and go his own way. He said, "Nothing is so much to be feared as fear. The sin that God hates is fear; he thinks Atheism innocent in comparison." He wrote in his diary: "If I do not keep step with others, it is because I hear a different drummer. Let a man step to the music which he hears, however measured, and however far away." He went to jail because he would not pay his poll-tax, on the ground that the government supported slavery. No one wanted to arrest him. The man who took him in custody offered himself to pay the tax. Judge Hoar in his charge to the jury, made what seems to me an ideal statement: "If a statute is passed which any citizen, examining his duty by the best light which God has given, . . . believes to be wicked, and which, acting under the law of God, he thinks he ought to disobey, unquestionably he ought to disobey that statute, because he ought to 'obey God rather than man.' . . . But . . . a man whose private conscience leads him to disobey a law recognised by the community must take the consequences of that disobedience. It is a matter solely between him and his Maker. . . . It will not do for the public authorities to recognise his private opinion as a justification of his acts." Mark Sabre himself could not have expressed the truth better than that.

From the year 1837 Thoreau kept a journal, which he wrote simply to please himself, not knowing that its contents would form permanent additions to American literature. He was careless of fame, publishing in his lifetime only two books—*A Week on the Concord and Merrimack Rivers* (1849) and *Walden* (1854), only two, *sed duo leones.* They were edited by himself from his diaries; after his death, his friends brought out a number of his works in the same manner, but although these supplementary volumes contain many interesting pages, the whole of Thoreau—the objective and subjective man—is to be found in the two books he saw through the press.

Thoreau will impress different readers very differently, and the same reader very differently in varying moods. One must love nature, freedom, independence, and understand the inner meaning of hyperbole and paradox, if one is to learn from Thoreau; and he has so much to teach us! For an unfavourable, unsympathetic, and unjust estimate of Thoreau, we may read the famous essay by James Russell Lowell; he never knew the man intimately, and perhaps would not have liked him anyhow. This essay is witty, shrewd, penetrating; but it misses its mark. Lowell had too much common sense, too much humour, too much urban polish, to appreciate either Thoreau's character or his doctrines. The best two books on the subject are the *Life of Thoreau* by F. B. Sanborn and the little volume called *Henry Thoreau as Remembered by a Young Friend,* by Edward Emerson.

The various portraits of Thoreau, those with and without the beard, are curiously interesting, because they seem to reveal the nature of the man. There is a look of both shyness and wildness. Strangers who met him always thought of some wild beast, wild, but not malignant. There is a look in the eyes such as I have seen in those of partridges in the woods, the instant before they fly.

When a man finds that he can be quite happy in solitude, and proclaims the fact, he is sure to be condemned. Society feels uncomfortable when informed of its superfluousness, or of its stupidity. The average man suspects that such men as Thoreau are dangerous, because so self-sufficient. He is not flattering to our self-esteem. Just as every suicide is a resounding vote against existence, so every rebel is a vote against organisation. Most people cannot hold political, social or religious beliefs with any comfort unless thousands of others share their faith. Thoreau is upsetting, disturbing, like a mosquito in the night. Many have decided that he is either negligible or a nuisance. He is still accused of conceit and selfishness. The moral watchword of the twentieth century, "Service," did not appeal to him. He was content to live in his own way, apart from all forms of community activity.

"God plants us where we grow," said Pompilia; and Thoreau could not grow unless there were trees around him. He accomplished much more for the world by living along with nature than by joining any Welfare Society. He has shown us the pleasures of the woods and streams, the marvels of nature to which we are blind and deaf, the possibility of simplicity of living, the enormous virtue of sincerity, the manly independence that comes from economy. His books are a greater blessing to humanity than if they had been conventional.

Thoreau's admirable literary style owes much to his sound cultural training. He was a fine Greek scholar, and deeply read in both Latin and French literature. There is a classic precision in his English, which he obtained partly from French models. Simplicity, clearness, adjectival accuracy—these are distinguishing qualities. There is a happy tendency to use short sentences. I remember a teacher telling us at school, "The glory of French prose is the short sentence."

Thoreau is Emerson's greatest pupil. Living in Emerson's household two years, it was inevitable that he should bear the stamp of that powerful mind, the most profound mind in American literature. People who met Thoreau at first thought he was an imitation of Emerson; they seemed to see a rough copy, even in voice and gesture. But when they became more intimately acquainted with the disciple, they found that his chief imitation of Emerson was in his absolute originality and independence, qualities common to both teacher and pupil. Emerson was an inspiration rather than a model. Thoreau's way of thinking, his peremptory challenges, his frank directness, his sturdy self-sufficiency, his love of paradox, were natural qualities which received further stimulation by close daily association with the man he loved. Even his economy—"lessen your denominator," is of course Emersonian.

His tendency to mysticism was heightened by Emerson's transcendentalism. Thoreau, like Wordsworth, believed in a spiritual Reality in Nature. He identifies himself with Walden Pond. Animals and so-called inanimate nature are part of the same essence of which he is composed. Thoreau was a deeply religious man, who believed in God and loved Him, and who in nature lived closer to Him than many professionally religious men. He seemed certain of the future life, so certain that he did not feel it necessary to be always talking or even thinking about it. His famous answer to a questioner about eternity was, "One world at a time."

The Personification of the Pond in *Walden* is one of the most memorable features of that extraordinary book. The Pond was his living, intimate friend, and he studied its surface as one watches the play of expression on the face of a human being. If a man must go away from towns and villages, a lake is not a bad partner; it is like a friend, who, loyal and steadfast at heart, is perpetually interesting in a variety of moods.

The perspective in Walden is particularly interesting. Just as the drawing in *Gulliver's Travels* is always according to scale, whether we are in Lilliput or Brobdingnag, so Walden is consistently and appropriately magnified. It is an ocean. Concord River is Lake Huron. A mud-puddle is an estuary.

The finest piece of writing in *Walden*, perhaps the finest in Thoreau, is the immortal battle of the ants. It is like a contest among Titans. It is as if he had turned a prodigious lens upon the struggling insects, and they had become monsters. No one could have written the account of the World War among the ants, unless he had been saturated in Homer, for the whole history is not only epic in range, breadth, and intensity, but is peculiarly Homeric in the elevation of heroes.

I was witness to events of a less peaceful character. One day when I went out to my wood-pile, or rather my pile of stumps, I observed two large ants, the one red, the other much larger, nearly half an inch long, and black, fiercely contending with one another. Having once got hold they never let go, but struggled and wrestled and rolled on the chips incessantly. Looking farther, I was surprised to find that the chips were covered with such combatants, that it was not a *duellum*, but a *bellum*, a war between two races of ants, the red always pitted against the black, and frequently two red ones to one black. The legions of these Myrmidons covered all the hills and vales in my woodyard, and the ground was already strewn with the dead and dying, both red and black. It was the only battle which I have ever witnessed, the only battlefield I ever trod while the battle was raging; internecine war; the red republicans on the one hand, and the black imperialists on the other. On every side they were engaged in deadly combat, yet without any noise that I could hear, and human soldiers never fought so resolutely. I watched a couple that were fast locked in each other's embrace, in a little sunny valley amid the chips, now at noon-day prepared to fight till the sun went down, or life went out. The smaller red champion had fastened himself like a vice to his adversary's front, and through all the tumblings on that field never for an instant ceased to gnaw at one of his feelers near the root, having already caused the other to go by the board; while the stronger black one dashed him from side to side, and, as I saw on looking nearer, had already divested him of several of his members. They fought with more pertinacity than bull-dogs. Neither manifested the least disposition to retreat. It was evident that their battle-cry was Conquer or die. In the meanwhile there came along a single red ant on the hillside of this valley, evidently full of excitement, who either had despatched his foe, or had not yet taken part in the battle; probably the latter, for he had lost none of his limbs; whose mother had charged him to return with his shield or upon it. Or perchance he was some Achilles, who had nourished his wrath apart, and had now come to avenge or rescue his Patroclus. He saw this unequal combat from afar,—for the blacks were nearly twice the size of the red,—he drew near with rapid pace till he stood on his guard within half an inch of the combatants, then, watching his opportunity, he sprang upon the black warrior, and commenced his operations near the root of his right fore-leg, leaving the foe to select among his own members; and so there were three united for life, as if a new kind of attraction had been invented which put all other locks and cements to shame. I should not have wondered by this time to find that they had their respective musical bands stationed on some eminent chip, and playing their national airs the while to excite the slow and cheer the dying combatants. I was myself excited somewhat even as if they had been men. The more you think of it, the less the difference. And certainly there is not the fight recorded in Concord history, at least, if in the history of America, that will bear a moment's comparison with this, whether for the numbers engaged in it, or for the patriotism and heroism displayed. For numbers and for carnage it was an Austerlitz or Dresden. Concord Fight! Two killed on the patriots' side, and Luther Blanchard wounded! Why here every ant was a Buttrick,—"Fire! for God's sake fire!"—and thousands shared the fate of Davis and Hosmer. There was not one hireling there. I have no doubt that it was a principle they fought for, as much as our ancestors, and not to avoid a threepenny tax on their tea; and the results of this battle will be as important and memorable to those whom it concerns as those of the battle of Bunker Hill, at least.

I took up the chip on which the three I have particularly described were struggling, carried it into my house, and placed it under a tumbler on my window-sill, in order to see the issue. Holding a microscope to the first mentioned red ant, I saw that, though he was assiduously gnawing at the near fore-leg of his enemy, having severed his remaining feeler, his own breast was all torn away, exposing what vitals he had there, to the jaws of the black warrior, whose breast-plate was apparently too thick for him to pierce; and the dark carbuncles of the sufferer's eyes shone with ferocity such as war only could excite. They struggled half an hour longer under the tumbler, and when I looked again the black soldier had severed the heads of his foes from their bodies, and the still living heads were hanging on either side of him like ghastly trophies at his saddle-bow, still apparently as firmly fastened as ever, and he was endeavouring with feeble struggles, being without feelers and with only the remnant of a leg, and I know not how many other wounds, to divest himself of them, which at length, after half an hour more, he accomplished. I raised the glass, and he went off over the window-sill in that crippled state. Whether he finally survived that combat, and spent the remainder of his days in some Hôtel des Invalides, I do not know; but I thought that his industry would not be worth much thereafter. I never learned which party was victorious, nor the cause of the war; but I felt for the rest of that day as if I had had my feelings excited and harrowed by witnessing the struggle, the ferocity and carnage, of a human battle before my door.

Such an account is not only thrilling in itself, but its irony is unmistakable. It is a kind of Universal History of Humanity, with an anti-patriotic bias. The chronicler never learned "the cause of the war."

Thoreau is the nearest modern approach to Diogenes. He lives alone in his tub, and rails at humanity, and at the busyness of the human race. Civilisation is all pointed in the wrong direction, he tells us. I should like it better if he had not insisted so much on his own happiness; sometimes I think he protests too much. I was glad when he admitted that along about two o'clock in the afternoon he often found it a bit dull. He became decivilised, inhuman in a harmless way. He heard the insistent call of the wild, and loved to revert to the savage type. There was primitive blood in him. I have often wondered how much of this in Thoreau was Mere Boy. Every schoolboy is at heart a savage. The love of the woods and wild life, the passion for vagabondage, the delight in leaving home comforts and fending for oneself,—it is in every boy's heart, and many have it long after they have put away other childish things. Think of the millions of people who "camp out every year—what makes them do it?

No literary man ever lived closer to nature than Thoreau. He was not a scientist, he was an observer. He may have made no new discoveries; but he discovered for us things that ought to be familiar, and are not. His minute, intimate knowledge of sights and sounds in the forest is uncanny. I think nearly all of his readers envy him this understanding. His woodcraft was perfect and every noise had a definite significance. These things are worth knowing, because they are a part of all life, like ourselves. In Thoreau's eyes there is nothing unimportant, nothing trivial; every thing, every event in nature has dignity.

No professor of pedagogy has begun to have the effect on modern primary education produced by the work of Thoreau.

Thoreau was not only a Naturalist and a Philosopher; he was a Poet. I do not refer to his published verses, which blossom in his books like wild flowers in a meadow; he was always bursting into rime, because his head was full of ancient and modern poetry, and his senses were attuned to musical rhythm.

He was devoted to music; loved to play, loved to sing, loved to dance. His verses are as natural as the singing of a bird. Yet, in the strict sense, he was not a poet, for he never wrote a first-rate poem. What I mean is that he was a poet at heart, and expressed himself in many ways besides the little rough-hewn verses that he composed. It was his poetical temperament that enabled him to live alone in the woods. He transfigured everything with the alchemy of his imagination. His enthusiasm at Springtide is contagious.

Had an unimaginative man attempted to live in the manner of Thoreau he would have gone mad; many solitary shepherds lose their reason. But Thoreau had endless resources in his own mind. His powers of observation were so sharp that on any walk he saw things hidden from the wise and prudent; and he was so filled with the best reading that he was himself a circulating library, with constant and immediate access to the shelves.

Lowell thought Thoreau had little humour, which was a curious error. It is true that to the average man Thoreau's actions seemed "funny," but not nearly so much so as the other way around. He secretly enjoyed the antics of human beings, in their mad pursuit of more money, in their excitement over politics, in their scramble up the social ladder, in their fights over dogma. The show amused him enormously. Furthermore he drew intense enjoyment out of the humourous side of nature. His observations sufficiently indicate this. The loon, the owl, the squirrels filled him repeatedly with silent laughter. He even enjoyed playing with fish, and treated their prejudices respectfully. "I have thus stood over them half an hour at a time, and stroked them familiarly without frightening them, suffering them to nibble my fingers harmlessly, and seen them erect their dorsal fins in anger when my hand approached their ova, and have even taken them gently out of the water with my hand. . . . Though stationary, they keep up a constant sculling or waving motion with their fins, which is exceedingly graceful, and expressive of their humble happiness."

Thoreau heartily disliked politics, the idea of the State, theological controversies, social distinctions; but he loved nature, music, and religion. His pair of sentences on music in the Merrimack book are exactly in harmony with Schopenhauer's philosophy and Browning's interpretations in *Abt Vogler*. Music is a deeper truth than any verbal expression. He says, "Music is the sound of the universal laws promulgated. It is the only assured tone. There are in it such strains as far surpass any man's faith in the loftiness of his destiny." Or, as Browning wrote, "The rest may reason and welcome: 'tis we musicians know."

It seems a far cry from the healthiness of Thoreau to the morbidity of Freud; but there is another passage in the book just quoted that if it were written now would be regarded as Freudian. "Dreams are the touchstones of our characters. We are scarcely less afflicted when we remember some unworthiness in our conduct in a dream, than if it had been actual, and the intensity of our grief, which is our atonement, measures inversely the degree by which this is separated from an actual unworthiness. For in dreams we but act a part which must have been learned and rehearsed in our waking hours, and no doubt could discover some waking consent thereto. If this meanness has not its foundation in us, why are we grieved at it? In dreams we see ourselves naked and acting out our real characters, even more clearly than we see others awake. But an unwavering and commanding virtue would compel even its most fantastic and faintest dreams to respect its ever wakeful authority; as we are accustomed to say carelessly, we should never have *dreamed* of such a thing. Our truest life is when we are in dreams awake."

Thoreau was a germinal writer, though few suspected it while he was alive. He lives to-day not only through his own books, but through those of John Burroughs, W. H. Hudson, and the ever-increasing number of nature writers, nature students, and also nature fakers. He would have been both amused and disgusted by the last, which are a kind of caricature, having the relation of alchemy to chemistry, astrology to astronomy, mediums to mystics.

Intellectually he was an anarchist. Some one has called him a "calm Nietzsche," and it was not until the writings of the latter became popular that Thoreau was translated into German (1897). But we need this particular kind of anarchist, who has no murder in his heart. He questions accepted dogmas, he questions our political ideals, he questions the activities that keep us from living. Just as I finished writing that sentence, I was interrupted by a telephone conversation on my income tax. This would have amused him.

Thoreau answered ridicule by searching the conscience. He said to an audience, "There's a good time coming, boys," and one of them asked, "Can you fix the date?" He replied, "Will you help it along?"

To read Thoreau is to live in healthy surroundings in good company. He reinforces his observations of nature with quotations from the best authors. He was deeply read in the great Elizabethans, the quaint seventeenth century men like Sir Thomas Browne, and he loved Chaucer as he loved sunshine. His remarks on the *Canterbury Tales* in *A Week* are the best kind of literary criticism. There is in his own style a wild, piney flavour. He was not afraid of using homely words.

Everybody ought to read Thoreau. We

need him for our soul's health. There is no writer more antiseptic.

If I myself have such an admiration for Thoreau, which I have sincerely and honestly expressed in this essay, it is the best of all tributes to his genius. For I suppose I am exactly the kind of man whom he would have regarded as a lost soul. I live indoors most of the time, I belong to all sorts of religious and philanthropic societies, I love to be with men, women, and children, I prefer the city to the country, and when I go outdoors, I would alas! rather play golf than take a solitary walk in the woods. I do not enjoy too much fresh air in the house, and I have never even adopted that modern fad of a sleeping-porch, preferring a comfortable bedroom. If I, without imitating Thoreau's habits, can find him interesting, charming, refreshing, stimulating, and inspiring, what must he be to those who share his ideas?

LOWELL

Lowell always seemed to do or to say exactly the right thing at the right time; it was characteristic of him that he selected the twenty-second of February as his birthday. He was an ideal patriot, an ideal American; he is worthy of the man who made the holiday. He entered the world in 1819, in excellent literary society, having as associates George Eliot, John Ruskin, Charles Kingsley, and Walt Whitman. Like Oliver Wendell Holmes, he was born at Cambridge, Massachusetts, and he was one of the few Americans who died in the house in which he was born. Like Holmes also, he was identified with Harvard both as student and professor. His father was a minister, pastor of a Boston church.

There are two reasons why so many men of letters have been sons of ministers. In

JAMES RUSSELL LOWELL

small towns and remote villages, the minister was often the only man of culture and education; his home was filled with books; it was a centre of refinement and of humanising influences. The services of the clergy to the general intellectual elevation of the community can hardly be overestimated. Furthermore, most ministers believe heartily in education; nearly every one is determined to give his children a better education than he had himself. It is curious that so many people attack ministers of the Gospel for being ignorant and hidebound, when there has never been any social class that has made such sacrifices to give their offspring the highest intellectual advantages. I have known all kinds of preachers, but never one who was not interested in the life of the mind.

Lowell's family was old and distinguished. The town Lowell was named after one of them; and among his relations are the two brothers and sister who have in the twentieth century added distinction to the name—President Lowell of Harvard, Percival Lowell the astronomer, and Amy Lowell the poet.

His mother was a woman of culture, fond of music, and an accomplished linguist. She and her son were not only intimate friends, they enjoyed mental companionship, and he respected her mind as much as he loved her. One of the numerous reasons why women should have a "higher education" is in order that they may live in the same atmosphere as their grown-up children. Many sons pet their mothers and have no respect for their opinions.

Young Lowell grew up in a library. He said, "I am a Bookman." And he was. He was a Bookman, not a Bookworm.

He was graduated from Harvard in the class of 1838. He hated mathematics and cut chapel systematically. It should be remembered that chapel was held at sunrise. In his Senior year he was elected Class Poet, but the Faculty would not permit him to read his poem at the Commencement exercises, as he was under discipline. He heaped coals of fire on Harvard when he read the splendid Harvard Commemoration Ode in 1865.

Harvard is fortunate in having among her graduates Lowell, Emerson, Thoreau, and Holmes—they established a literary tradition of imponderable value, which is a permanent influence.

He was graduated from the Harvard Law School in 1840, but soon "abandoned the law for literature," his first volume of poems appearing when he was twenty-two. In 1851 he sailed for Europe, and spent months in Italy; on the return voyage in 1852 he had as shipmates Thackeray and Clough. In 1854 he was appointed Professor of Modern Languages at Harvard, succeeding Longfellow, and taught for twenty years. The best account of his manner in the classroom is given in Barrett Wendell's interesting essay, *Lowell as a College Teacher*. He was casual, and shocked the students by wearing a tall hat and a sack coat. Professor Beers entered his classroom one day, and reports that at the close of the lecture, a student asked Lowell for his mark on the exams. "What do *you* think you ought to have?" asked the professor. The student suggested a figure, which was gratefully adopted, the teacher saying, "That will save me the trouble of reading your paper."

In 1857, when the *Atlantic Monthly* was founded, Lowell became the first editor, combining that with his professional duties, as in a later day was done by Bliss Perry. He was subsequently editor of the *North American Review*. In 1877 he was appointed Minister to Spain, keeping up the Irving tradition; from 1880 to 1884 he was Minister to England. While our men are not trained for diplomacy as Europeans are, we have sent some fine representatives to foreign courts—Andrew White, Joseph Choate, Maurice Francis Egan, John Hay, Brand Whitlock, Thomas Nelson Page, Walter H. Page, and others. Lowell performed invaluable services to America during his residence in England. He elevated foreign opinion of his native land by illustrating in his own person, especially by his remarkable addresses, the cultivated Yankee. His notable essay, *Democracy,* was first delivered in Great Britain. I can remember when the yellow press called him pro-British, un-American, because he was so much admired abroad.

He died in his house Elmwood, at Cambridge, on 12 August 1891. On 22 February 1892, a notable memorial service was held in his honour in Appleton Chapel, attended by the most distinguished men in America.

There was no address, both Professor Child and Professor Norton believing that the service should consist entirely of music. Fortunately for me, one of the invited guests failed at the last moment, and I walked in with Oliver Wendell Holmes, who carried easily his eighty-two years. It was an impressive service, with no speaking and no reading, but with magnificent vocal music.

I had often seen Lowell walking in his grounds at Elmwood and I contributed one more paving-stone to the infernal regions by having the intention to seek an introduction to him, as was promised me by a friend. But I decided to wait until the autumn, and as a consequence I am waiting still.

Lowell was a bookman to the last. During his final illness, Holmes called one day, and asked, "James, how do you feel?" "I haven't the slightest idea," said Lowell, "I am reading Rob Roy."

Lowell was famous for three accomplishments which are just outside the field of pure literature—public speaking, letter-writing, and conversation. There are in America today probably more men who excel in the first than in the second, and more who excel in the second than in the third. It would be well if children could be brought up to practice conversation as a fine art, as in the eighteenth century; we have one hundred who can dance to one who can talk.

Lowell first became known, not as an imaginative poet, but as a humourist and satirist. In 1846 his *Biglow Papers* began to appear in the *Boston Courier* and were received in New England communities with enthusiasm. The Mexican War was exceedingly unpopular in our Eastern States; the majority of citizens were angry and chafing with suppressed rage and disgust. Lowell's dialect verses relieved the overcharged public mind by giving it free and full expression. His attitude toward the Mexican War was followed in a similar manner over half a century later by "Mr. Dooley," in his satires on the Spanish War. One used Yankee, the other Irish dialect, but both had the same aim, to make the war ridiculous. The United States as a nation has taken part in seven wars, and in only one of them—the Great War—has the country really been united.

From 1840 to 1846, Lowell had written serious and sentimental poetry. Now he came out in a new rôle. The exponent of Harvard culture spoke Yankee dialect, and spoke it to some purpose. The *Biglow Papers* are the most original of all his work, and positively glow with vitality. Hawthorne represented Puritanism, Longfellow domestic Americanism, Lowell Yankeeism. No one would have thought it possible to make "real poetry" out of Yankee ideas and sentiments, still less out of Yankee dialect, but Lowell achieved his purpose. He represented the four main traits of the typical Yankee—Shrewdness, Caution, Humour, Moral Principle. Lowell was as stern a follower of duty as Emerson, but he expressed his sentiments in a quite different style. If there is anything in Lowell beyond highly developed talent—if there is in his work the spark of genius—it is to be found in the *Biglow Papers.* They are not merely clever and facile, like the work of Holmes; they are the product of native genius. They came straight out of Yankee soil, and their author was the spokesman of New England. He was less than thirty when he wrote them; they sparkle with the brilliance and audacity of youth. If the subject, the Mexican War, had not been so local, it is probable that the *Biglow Papers* would be classed among the great satires in the literature of the world. They are written with the splendid ease that characterises Dryden's *Absalom and Achitophel,* Butler's *Hudibras,* Pope's *Dunciad,* Byron's *English Bards and Scotch Reviewers.*

As dialect poems, they have a quite special value. The dialect is perfect, but it isn't the essential thing, as in Tennyson's *Northern Farmer.* Dialect should never be used if it is possible not to use it. Dialect is a means, not an end. Dialect is simply italic type, it is a method of emphasis; it brings the object or the speaker to us with sharper delineation. That is why dialect is so well adapted for purposes of caricature. Caricature, by the overemphasis of certain features, makes the object more real than a photograph.

Dialect is mimicry. It is not easy to explain exactly where lies the humour in mimicry; but we all feel it. We feel it mildly when we put a pair of spectacles and a bonnet on a dog, we feel it strongly when some rather ridiculous person is perfectly imitated. It is largely of course the element of the incongruous but I don't think that is a complete explanation. The subject is worth thinking about.

The *Biglow Papers* will be forever a record of Yankee dialect. Lowell used it properly, artistically, to emphasise his points; to make the poems picturesque; to represent more dramatically the Yankee attitude; to make it truly representative of the common people; to add the touch of humour, which, as we have seen, is in all accurate mimicry.

The moral effect of the poems was tremendous. They stirred up Northern feeling against slavery, and against war. The fundamental appeal was not to the sense of humour, but to the conscience. Lowell's pen in both series was mightier than the sword. He attacked the Mexican War with the weapon of ridicule, and laughed at the organised sentimentality which has been found necessary in all wars. Furthermore, he declared war to be incompatible with Christianity.

Thet air flag's a leetle rotten,
  Hope it aint your Sunday's best;—
Fact! it takes a sight o' cotton
  To stuff out a soger's chest:
Sence we farmers hev to pay fer't,
  Ef you must wear humps like these,
S'posin' you should try salt hay fer't,
  It would du ez slick ez grease.

Ez fer war, I call it murder,—
  There you hev it plain an' flat;
I don't want to go no furder
  Than my Testyment fer that;
God hez sed so plump an' fairly,
  It's ez long ez it is broad,
An' you've gut to git up airly
  Ef you want to take in God.

Here is an interesting question. Had Lowell published this poem in the spring of 1917, he would have been sent to prison for twenty years, and treated as a traitor. Why was it possible to publish it in 1846? Why was it possible in 1898 for Mr. Dooley to ridicule the war with Spain? Why was it possible for Professor W. G. Sumner, when the Spanish War was at its height, to deliver a public lecture called *The Conquest of the United States by Spain,* and be never mobbed, deprived of his professorship, or sent to jail?

Well, there are among others, two reasons. First, in the wars with Mexico and Spain, our country was not in any physical danger, however great the danger to her soul. Second, there was plenty of local sentiment to support the attitude of opposition. It is local sentiment that invariably determines the enforcement of any law and the safety of public speech and the freedom of private opinion. Lloyd George, John Morley, and G. K. Chesterton made public speeches against the South African War when it was raging; and although they were mobbed, there was no thought of sending them to prison.

Lowell paid his compliments in this same poem to the yellow press. It is curious that everyone who shouts for war while we are at peace is called a patriot, and is physically safe; whereas those who attempt to prevent the declaration of war are called public enemies, and are in serious peril.

Take them editors thet's crowin'
  Like a cockerel three months old,—
Don't ketch any on 'em goin',
  Though they be so blasted bold;
Aint they a prime lot o' fellers?
  'Fore they think on't guess they'll sprout
(Like a peach thet's got the yellers),
  With the meanness bustin' out.

In the last stanza, Lowell, like so many Northern Abolitionists, declared his preference for secession.

Ef I'd my way I hed ruther
  We should go to work an' part,

They take one way, we take t'other,
  Guess it wouldn't break my heart;
Man hed ough' to put asunder
  Them that God has noways jined;
An' I shouldn't gretly wonder
  Ef there's thousands o' my mind.

If this was treason, nobody seemed inclined to make the most of it. The poem was greeted with rapturous acclaim; everybody wanted more of the same thing, and got it.

We were gittin' on nicely up here to our village,
  With good old ideas o' wut's right an' wut aint,
We kind o' thought Christ went again war an' pillage,
  An' thet eppyletts worn't the best mark of a saint;
      But John P.
      Robinson he
Sez this kind o' thing's an exploded idee.

Parson Wilbur sez he never heered in his life
  That th' Apostles rigged out in their swaller-tail coats,
An' marched round in front of a drum an' a fife,
  To git some on 'em office, an' some on 'em votes;
      But John P.
      Robinson he
Sez they didn't know everythin' down in Judee.

A note was added, supposedly written by Parson Wilbur, in which was attacked the "pernicious" sentiment, "Our country, right or wrong." . . . "There is a patriotism of the soul whose claim absolves us from our other and terrene fealty. . . . That is a hard choice when our earthly love of country calls upon us to tread one path and our duty points to another." This is indeed a perplexing question with independent thinkers—shall they follow the truth of abstract principle or the truth of loyalty? Shall a man who believes that war is murder uphold war in certain conditions? Well, Lowell, like many other honest men, was forced in 1861 to compromise with his convictions, and take what seemed to be the lesser of the two evils. Happy are those who are untroubled by principles, or to whom the supreme principle is *Our Country, right or wrong.*

It is at any rate a defensible proposition, that if a man believes a case to be fifty-one percent right, he should give it one hundred percent of his support. It is an imperfect world, and we must act in it on that understanding; for not to act at all is in itself an eloquent action. I think it was Hegel who said that in most cases conscientious people cannot choose between black and white; they must choose between dark brown and light brown. All I know is that they must choose.

In the Second Series, published during the Civil War, Lowell was ardently patriotic. Nor was there any loss of power; they were as brilliant, forceful, and ingenious as the earlier satires. The situation was so much graver that the poems took on a deeper intensity. And the dialect added to their effect. Charles Sumner said he wished "the author of the *Biglow Papers* could have used good English." That was an appalling criticism. Yet there are times when the moral sentiments seen grotesquely clad.

There is another and gentler side to the *Biglow Papers* which gave pleasure to all and offence to none. They belong to pastoral literature. The pastoral side of New England life is as clearly and fully presented as Sicilian life in Theocritus, or Roman life in Virgil. *The Courtin'* is decidedly superior to the average of pastorals in the English language. The scent of the New England hayfield, sometimes of the barnyard, hovers over these verses. The American eagle becomes a domestic fowl. *The Courtin'* is an American classic, and might be called a Yankee Eclogue.

The prose part of the *Biglow Papers* is too minute and too diffuse, though these qualities count in the general satirical effect. If read in separate papers, they are more effective than in their final book form. They contain specimens of the author's wit, and reveal the richness of his mind. Only a man of culture could have produced them. They contain satires on the newspapers as autocrats of good English; on ignorant purists, whose pedantry is equalled only by lack of culture; they show Lowell's fondness for vital colloquialisms, and their allusiveness indicates the range of his reading. They are full of sound common sense, humour and ideality.

In both serious and conventional poetry, Lowell is decidedly unequal. He lacked technique and final finish. The language is seldom inevitable as it so often is in Keats and in Tennyson. He never wrote a flawless poem like the *Ode on a Grecian Urn* or *Ulysses.*

The *Fable for Critics,* written just for fun

and tripping along in easy doggerel, is chiefly valuable to-day as genuine criticism of American authors in the year 1848. It has a fatal fluency that carries the author often into waste places; but it is witty, humourous, and kindly. It is notably free from any suspicion of envy, and the criticism directed against his own work was just. To go back to its prototype we should have to read Suckling's *Sessions of the Poets,* a commentary on seventeenth century writers. Would that every age of literature had a *Fable for Critics* written by a competent hand! There was one published in 1922, but its inferiority to the other is its chief characteristic.

His poems are marred by sentimentality and moralising, the two most prominent defects in American literature. Tennyson's *Poems of 1842* had a powerful influence on Americans of that generation, and their sentimentality was more contagious than their splendour. *Sir Launfal,* beautiful as it is, is over sentimentalised, which perhaps is the reason why it has ever been a hot favourite with youthful readers. As he advanced in years, Lowell's verses carried more freight.

There is a broader and deeper foundation of thought, with occasionally a weighty line, like

God's passionless reformers, influences.

He learned how to combine thought-strength with word-strength. *After the Burial* is sincere and impressive.

He reached his climax in the noble *Harvard Commemoration Ode* of 1865. For once a poet was worthy of a great occasion. His style was equal to his theme. This Ode has perhaps with justice been called "the most important contribution that the Civil War has made to song." It is one of the finest Odes in the English language, superior even to Tennyson's Ode on the Death of the Duke of Wellington. The Ode, as a form of poetic expression, has gone out of fashion, being almost as obsolete as Tragedy; but this will remain as a particularly fine specimen of a lost art. The author was inspired, and wrote it in a few hours. The burning sincerity, the passionate conviction, found free expression in boldly metaphorical language. The joy of victory was shadowed by the death of Lincoln, and the tribute to him is the finest thing in the poem. It pronounced a judgment that the years have ratified.

As a poet Lowell never reached the technical perfection of Poe, the solemn adagio music of Bryant, the curious concreteness and insight of Emerson, the romantic picturesqueness of Longfellow, the elemental shock of Whitman. But he had a larger and richer poetical endowment than any of these; and with all his faults, his poetry is satisfying to men who value ideas and masculine force.

Lowell was an Elizabethan personality, as Holmes was Augustan. He united in his nature something of three Elizabethans—Spenser, Sidney, Raleigh. He had Spenser's dreamy romanticism, Sidney's knightly idealism, Raleigh's virile earnestness. He is like the Elizabethans in his overflowing vitality, in his essential manliness.

He was preeminently a man of Ideas rather than a man of Thought, like Emerson, or a man of Facts, like Franklin. His sense of humour kept him from a world of abstraction—perhaps kept him from the heights of poetry.

Lowell was ambidextrous, like Poe, Emerson, and Holmes. He achieved equal distinction in both verse and prose. Just as I prefer Emerson's verse to his prose, so I prefer Lowell's prose to his verse. One of his favourite authors was Dryden, and although Dryden was a professional poet, it is his prose that we read with the keener interest. Like Dryden's, Lowell's genius was more naturally fitted for prose expression, because the two chief elements in his nature were strength and freedom. He hated fetters. His prose has some of the best qualities of extempore speech, where there are frequent flashes of inspiration.

His essays show a combination of the creative and critical faculties. This is rather remarkable, because the critical instinct is apt to sterilise the creative, as can be seen in such men of genius as Lessing, Thomas Gray, Matthew Arnold and Henry James. Lowell's essays on Dryden, on Chaucer, and on Democracy are primarily creative. It is not necessary that the original author should have intended what the critic sees in his work; it is the true critic's business not only to interpret his author to the public, but to use him as a quarry for ideas. (On this particular subject, nothing more suggestive has been written than the work by Oscar Wilde, called *Intentions,* containing the article on *The Critic as Artist.)*

Lowell's prose has from certain points of view the same merits and defects so evident in his verse, because it bears the same impress. There is an exuberance of power. Most books, like most men, lack energy; here we have freshness, health, vigour, abounding force. Such qualities produce fundamental virtues and surface faults. As he shocked Barrett Wendell by wearing a tall hat over a sack coat, so his flashes of irrepressible humour shocked some formalities. They forgot that

> Frothy spume and frequent sputter
> Prove that the soul's depths boil in earnest!

When he said that Milton got poetry out of a cataract, and meant the one in his eye, he displeased those who did not like that sort of thing. Lowell's audacity was continually cropping out. His mind was in constant eruption. All sorts of metaphors and similes were continually rising to the surface, from spontaneous combustion. Sometimes they become mere "conceits," in the manner of the

Metaphysical School of the seventeenth century. Oftener they are precisely happy. The essay *Democracy* may be profitably studied from this point of view. By the way, has anyone ever given a more fruitful definition of Superstition than there occurs? "Superstition, by which I mean the respecting of that which we are told to respect, rather than that which is respectable in itself." In the brilliant essay on Gray, speaking of the comfortable minds of the eighteenth century, he said, "Responsibility for the universe had not then been invented."

Lowell was splendidly equipped for the profession of critic. He had the armoury of ancient, mediæval, and modern literature at his command. His essay on Chaucer reveals the qualities necessary for its undertaking. He knew Chaucer's poetry and Chaucer's language with a scholar's knowledge. He knew the literature of the fourteenth century, both in England and in Europe. He had that sympathy with humanity which no scholarship, however necessary, could on this theme be by itself a sufficient preparation. He had learning without pedantry. Woodrow Wilson has defined pedantry as being "out of touch with life," (and by the irony of fate, no statesman has been oftener called a pedant than he). Although Lowell could not help revealing his learning, he never made a pedantic display. He possessed his knowledge; it did not possess him. He wore his learning like a graceful garment, rather than a clumsy coat of mail; for there are learned writers who move as awkwardly as David in Saul's armour. What should be a help is a hindrance. The moment you open a book by Lowell, you feel at ease, as a stranger does in the presence of a gentleman. He puts his reader on a familiar footing, as an intimate public speaker does his audience.

Lowell was rather fond of long sentences, but they did not cumber the ground. He was never ponderous or involved. His paragraphs are composed of well-trained phrases, all under discipline. They move together like a perfectly-drilled line of soldiers in battle-array, in heavy marching order, their ranks gleaming with bayonets.

His sense of fact and his sense of humour were so strong that while they helped him to appreciate certain authors, they acted in other instances as a limitation. He never understood Thoreau, and I think he would have been surprised could he have known the exalted position held by the woodsman in the twentieth century. He was at times unjust to Carlyle, and when he wrote the essay on Milton, he thought the monumental Life by Masson simply funny.

Apart from his learning and his literary genius, Lowell's critical essays carry conviction because their author was always a man first, and a scholar second. Knowledge of life is an essential qualification for a literary critic, and no amount of learning can atone for the lack of it. When I was a sophomore in college, I was requested by the professor to write a theme on the subject—"Does Sophocles represent Oedipus as suffering for sin?" First I sat down and reread *Oedipus the King* in Greek—read it from beginning to end, with spinal thrills. Then I decided to see what the scholars had written about it. I read a number of essays by famous professors and specialists, and they seemed to me to know ever so much more about the Greek language than about human nature. Finally I read a criticism by the Irishman Mahaffy that was full of blood.

Some years later I had a memorable conversation with him at three o'clock in the morning. I told him of my disappointment in those learned treatises, and asked him what was the matter. "The matter is," said he, "that those men you mention know nothing about life. They have spent their days with their noses in books, and their nights under a lamp."

In other words, these gentlemen and others of the same breed are unfitted for literary criticism. Does not this simple fact explain the futility of most of the commentaries on the great authors of ancient and modern times? When I think of the annotations on Shakespeare that I have seen put forward seriously by serious scholars, and know while reading them that a shrewd man of the world could do better, I am reenforced in my conviction that sympathy with life is the prime prerequisite for literary criticism. Literature is the immortal part of history; literature is the essence of life. How is it possible for a man to understand the character of Falstaff if equipped only with a knowledge of Elizabethan English? When a German commentator said that Falstaff should not be admired because he was untrustworthy, is not such a remark a revelation of ignorance more blank than if he had misunderstood some of the words?

Poetry and drama were not written in order that they might be used as textbooks in schools, or to give employment to pedants, but because their authors felt the imperious need of self-expression, and got relief by the interpretation of men and women. To know nothing about life, to have small sympathy with the passions, sins, and weaknesses of human nature, is therefore to be as grotesquely unfitted for literary scholarship as to attempt to be a civil engineer with no knowledge of mathematics.

Lowell's humanity shines through everything he wrote. His fine scholarship was simply a magnifying glass, which would have helped him not at all if he had been blind.

Lowell was once thought to be our greatest man of letters. Few would give him that supreme position to-day, and what his position in the twenty-first century will be, is problematical. But he is our most versatile writer. He was a wit, a humorist, a satirist, an essayist, a critic, a master of dialect, a poet.

When he stood before an English audience and defended the highest ideals of democracy, he was himself an incarnation of those ideals. As Sir Philip Sidney was the finest type of monarchical gentleman, so James Russell Lowell will remain, in word and in deed, in accomplishment and in character, the finest representative of the modern republican gentleman.

HENRY JAMES

JAMES

Henry James was born in New York, 15 April 1843, and died in London, 28 Febuary 1916. He must be reckoned among the casualties of the Great War; there is no doubt that the tremendous interest he took in the struggle, his passionate partisanship of the cause of the Allies, his anxiety, exposure and wakefulness, were contributing factors to his taking off. It is a pity that he did not live to see the close of the struggle; but what he would think of the present situation in the year of grace 1923 is as problematical as the situation itself.

His parentage and education were as happy for his career as those of Robert Browning and John Stuart Mill. Metropolitan and cosmopolitan, he was born in a huge city, he never knew the tragic frustrations of poverty, and his father, in all intellectual matters, was the incarnation of an interrogation point. The family conversation that encircled his infancy was stimulating; even had he never left American shores, his boyhood mentally would have been quite different from that of the normal snuffly child. Children that are brought up chiefly on motion pictures and automobiles are bound to be intellectually incompetent, no matter how healthy in body, or amiable in disposition.

Had his father determined that young Henry should become a man of letters, he could hardly have given him a better education. He enjoyed the advantages of a long sojourn in Europe, learning foreign languages, worshipping all forms of true art, and measuring human endeavour by the highest standards. He never had to get rid of the thick prejudices caused by philistinism and provincialism; for he never breathed anything but the purest intellectual air. In nearly every instance, the advance towards maturity consists fully as much in shaking off falsenesses as in acquiring truths. The process of unlearning was, in the case of Henry James, almost negligible.

His only contact with young America in

the mass consisted of a brief residence at the Harvard Law School; and he, like innumerable others, "abandoned law for literature."

To the unregenerate Philistine, the life and talents of Henry James were wasted. He showed little interest in questions of politics, finance, business, sociology, morality, or religion. Until the Great War broke out in 1914, he was never a partisan, and looked on at the political game with irony. He regarded an artistic career as more dignified than entering Congress or Parliament. In nounces his intention of becoming an actor, his family are scandalised, and suggest that he might enter politics, to which he replies, "but comedian for comedian, isn't the actor on rather a higher plane?"

In *The Bostonians* (1886) the most satirical of his novels, he holds up to continuous ridicule women who are obsessed by political and social activities, charity work, social betterment work, everything that goes under the name of "uplift." His views on Woman Suffrage never needed to be stated after the publication of that book, and although it was one of his novels, when a young man an-omitted from the New York edition of his

Collected Works, it may be that some militant suffragette had read it and remembered it, when she slashed his portrait with a knife. In this same novel, his hero, who plainly carries the sympathy of his creator, speaks of American literature in terms reechoed two years ago by Joseph Hergesheimer.

> I am so far from thinking, as you set forth the other night, that there is not enough woman in our general life, that it has long been pressed home to me that there is a great deal too much. The whole generation is womanised; the masculine tone is passing out of the world; it's a feminine, a nervous, hysterical, chattering, canting age, an age of hollow phrases and false delicacy and exaggerated solicitudes and coddled sensibilities, which, if we don't soon look out, will usher in the reign of mediocrity, of the feeblest and flattest and the most pretentious that has ever been. The masculine character, the ability to dare and endure, to know and yet not fear reality, to look the world in the face and take it for what it is—a very queer and partly very base mixture—that is what I want to preserve, or rather, as I may say, to recover; and I must tell you that I don't in the least care what becomes of you ladies while I make the attempt!

The Great War changed his mental attitude, as it did that of so many others. Instead of being interested only in artistic matters, he gave himself, mind, heart, and soul to the struggle. Although he had not taken any real interest in American politics, he had never transferred his citizenship, and he would surely have died an American citizen if it had not been for the war. Some narrow-minded Americans have condemned him for becoming legally an Englishman. I think it was one of the noblest acts of his life. America had not entered the war; he had lived mainly in England; he was too old to enlist; and in order to identify himself completely with the cause, he transferred his allegiance from America to England. If this had cost him nothing, if he had really wanted to do it, he would have taken this step many years earlier; but it was because it cost him so much, because it was so great a sacrifice, that he felt an impelling necessity to do it only when England was in danger. For my part, I heartily applaud his conduct.

The letters written from August 1914, to his death in 1916, show a new Henry James. The cool observer becomes the passionate lover, the passionate hater. For the first time in his life, he was stirred to the depths of his nature by sentiments that had nothing to do with Art.

When the Editor of the *Yale Review* asked him to write an article as a cosmopolitan, he received the following reply:

> Let me say further that if I *were* miraculously able to give you something it wouldn't proceed at all, I think, from my "point of view as a cosmopolitan" (though indeed I'm not sure what that point of view at this hour can possibly be). I should speak altogether as a devoted friend to the Allies and an absolutely unrestricted participant in their cause—this is all my cosmopolitanism. But I daresay it's the state of mind you refer to after all, and I am faithfully yours.

Leaving out those last two years, Henry James, from the age of twenty to the age of seventy, was a writer of novels, short stories, literary essays; and he was nothing else. Few men have ever been able to give themselves so completely to a chosen profession. He was never married; he had enough money to keep him from the necessity of earning any, and not enough to employ his mind and time in taking care of it. He felt no obligations to citizenship, or to any form of religious, moral, or charitable work. He knew he was good for just one thing—literature; and if he ever questioned his moral responsibilities in the matter, there is no doubt that he completely justified himself. After all, in order to appreciate his attitude, one must oneself be convinced of the vital importance of Art in its relation to Life; and one must remember that in any other occupation, Henry James would have been a good deal worse than useless.

I am not surprised that those who care little for literature should feel a sense of futility in the ardours of Henry James; such depreciation is entirely natural. But the most bitter attack ever made against him came not from a business man or evangelist, but from a *novelist*—one for whom James had often expressed the liveliest affection and appreciation; the attack was therefore received by James with as much bewilderment as pain; his protesting letter is really an elaboration of the cry *et tu Brute!*

No two men could be more unlike in temperament than Henry James and H. G. Wells. The former believed that Art carried its own justification; the latter was always an "applied" artist, using his powers as a novelist to further some cause of economic or social betterment. Wells is a propagandist, which James was emphatically not. The exchange of letters between the two illuminates the whole questions of the relation of Art to life

When Wells published *Boon,* in which James was ridiculed he (rather strangely) sent a copy to his victim, and on 6 July 1915, James wrote him a letter from which the following extracts are significant:

> I have more or less mastered your appreciation of H. J., which I have found very curious and interesting after a fashion—though it has naturally not filled me with a fond elation. It is difficult of course for a writer to put himself *fully* in the place of another writer who finds him extraornarily futile and void, and who is moved to publish that to the world—and I think the case isn't easier when he happens to have enjoyed the other writer enormously from far back. . . . I am aware of certain things I have, and not less conscious, I believe, of various others that I am simply reduced to wish I did or could have; so I try, for possible light, to enter into the feelings of a critic for whom the deficiencies so preponderate. . . . I don't mean to say I don't wish I could do twenty things I can't—many of which you do so livingly; but I confess I ask myself what would become in that case of some of those to which I am most ad-

dicted and by which interest seems to me most beautifully producible. I hold that interest may be, *must* be, exquisitely made and created, and that if we don't make it, we who undertake to, nobody and nothing will make it for us; though nothing is more possible, nothing may even be more certain, than that my quest of it, my constant wish to run it to earth, may entail the sacrifice of certain things that are not on the straight line of it. However, there are too many things to say, and I don't think your chapter is really inquiring enough to entitle you to expect all of them.

To which missive Wells replied, 8 July 1915.

There is of course a real and very fundamental difference in our innate and developed attitudes towards life and literature. To you literature, like painting, is an end; to me literature, like architecture, is a means, it has a use. . . . I had rather be called a journalist than an artist, that is the essence of it, and there was no other antagonist possible than yourself. But since it was printed I have regretted a hundred times that I did not express our profound and incurable difference and contrast with a better grace.

Henry James replied to this letter at length, on 10 July. A few sentences must be quoted.

Of course for myself I live, live intensely and am fed by life, and my value, whatever it be, is in my own kind of expression of that. . . . Meanwhile I absolutely dissent from the claim that there are any differences whatever in the amenability to art of forms of literature aesthetically determined, and hold your distinction between a form that is (like) painting and a form that is (like) architecture for wholly null and void. There is no sense in which architecture is aesthetically "for use" that doesn't leave any other art whatever exactly as much so; and so far from that of literature being irrelevant to the literary report upon life, and to its being made as interesting as possible, I regard it as relevant in a degree that leaves everything else behind. It is art that *makes* life, makes interest, makes importance, for our consideration and application of these things, and I know of no substitute whatever for the force and beauty of its process. If I were Boon I should say that any pretence of such a substitute is helpless and hopeless humbug; but I wouldn't be Boon for the world, and am only yours faithfully,

HENRY JAMES.

Although the attack by his old friend caused Henry James much anguish, we may from a certain point of view be grateful for the onslaught; for it called forth an *apologia* by which we learn not only that our novelist believed in his work, but that he believed in it with his whole soul; hence there was fully as much consecration in his devotion to novel-writing, as there was in the preaching of Savonarola.

The manner of Henry James was as irritating to H. G. Wells as the results of it; when the posthumous work appeared, and the methods of the American novelist were given to the world, Wells made the angry and impatient comment, "he invites us to take a bath in his own sweat." The two men were so irreconcilably opposed in everything that it is a wonder the break between them was so long delayed.

It is interesting and creditable that while Henry James was so sensitive to criticism that he requested his publisher to send him no reviews at all, because the adverse ones hurt him so much that he thought it best to read none, he should have never made the slightest compromise to please the public. He was an affectionate, lovable man; he would have enjoyed popularity and a huge public; he knew that the course he elected was certain to deprive him of a multitude of readers; but so far from "writing down," so far from making his work "easy," so far from showing any amenity, he grew more and more difficult as he advanced in years. The last novel that appeared in his lifetime, *The Outcry,* I find absolutely unreadable. I went into training for it, like an athlete before a race; I got myself into good physical and mental condition, and then I attacked it with all the force I possessed. Yet although it is a short novel, I was stuck fast about half-way through, and found myself in an impenetrable thicket. I cannot, however, withhold admiration; there is something magnificent in the spectacle of an artist following the path of alienation, because it was the only path that satisfied his own ideals. He would have delighted in popularity; but he valued more than that his self-respect.

Despite his immense and ever-growing fame—there is not the slightest doubt that he is one of the giants in modern literature—his books have never had a wide circulation. Had he depended on the income from his novels for his financial support, he would have starved. Whether they were published serially or in book form made little difference; they were received by the few with rapture, and by the many with neglect.

The only time he endeavoured to capture the public was by a form of art for which he was singularly unfitted; he was predestined to failure. Anyone could have told him that. I refer to his pathetic attempts to write successful stage-plays. The whole melancholy story appears in his *Letters,* and his disappointment was keen. In the *Literary Supplement* of the *London Times* for 17 May 1923, Bernard Shaw gives the following interesting explanation:

The explanation is simple enough. There is a literary language which is perfectly intelligible to the eye, yet utterly unintelligible to the ear even when it is easily speakable by the mouth. Of that English James was master in the library and slave on the stage. At the last-mentioned performance I experimented on my friends between the acts by repeating some of the most exquisite sentences from the dialogue. I spoke fairly and distinctly, but not one of my victims could understand me or even identify the words I was uttering.

I cannot give any rule for securing audible intelligibility. It is not missed through long words or literary mannerisms or artificiality of style, nor secured by simplicity. Most of the dialogues that have proved effective on the English stage have been written either in the style of Shakespeare, which is often Euphuistic in its artificiality, or in that of Dr. Johnson, which is, as Goldsmith said, a style natural only to a whale. Ben Jonson's *Volpone* is detestably unreadable; yet, when spoken on the stage it is a model of vivid dialogue. The Jamesian passages with which I experimented did not contain any word of more than two syllables; word for word they were as simple as *The Pilgrim's Progress.* But they "came across" as gibberish. Speech does not differ from literature in its materials. "This my hand will rather the multitudinous seas incarnadine" is such a polysyllabic montrosity as was never spoken anywhere but on the stage; but it is magnificently effective and perfectly intelligible in the theatre. James could have paraphrased it charmingly in words of one syllable and left the audience drearily wondering what on earth Macbeth was saying.

Yet, curiously enough, Henry James ardently believed that his so-called "obscurities" would vanish if he were intelligently read aloud. He told me once that he had never written a sentence in his life that he did not mean to be read aloud, that he did not specifically intend to meet that test. "You try it and see." We know also that his later novels were dictated, whereas the earlier ones were written; and the more he dictated the more unintelligible he became.

Since his death, the student of his work

has had every opportunity to study the beginning and close of his career. The book reviews that he wrote in the early twenties have been collected and published in a volume called *Notes and Reviews.* Three volumes of his earliest short stories, *Travelling Companions, A Landscape Painter,* and *Master Eustace,* have been rescued from the magazines where they first appeared; two unfinished posthumous novels, *The Ivory Tower,* and *The Sense of the Past,* have been printed, accompanied by his notes for their continuance, which throw a flood of light on his slow, detailed method of work; and an autobiographical fragment, *The Middle Years,* is highly significant. In addition to these books, we have the *Letters* in two volumes, and also the *Letters* of his brother William; so that the materials for a final and complete study of the novelist are abundant.

The superb New York edition of his Works, in twenty-six tall and beautifully printed volumes, is also invaluable to the student, on account of the long and detailed prefaces which he supplied for every story, in which he takes the reader into his confidence.

I think no one admires the genius of

Henry James more than I—and I may add that I had and have the warmest affection and admiration for the man. It was impossible to talk with him and not be tremendously impressed both by his genius and by the winsome lovableness of his character and disposition. He had indeed a beautiful nature, as unspoiled as a child's. Yet I suppose I cannot be ranked among the devotees, for the simple reason that I think his nineteenth century novels incomparably superior to those of the twentieth. It is vain to prophesy, but I am confident that his fame will eventually rest on the earlier books. There will always be a few to whom *The Ambassadors* and *The Golden Bowl* will be a delight; and I should think a novelist might enjoy them technically. But I may myself never reread those; whereas the novels written in the 'seventies I hope to reread many times.

I am therefore incompetent to address those who prefer the later novels; I am entirely willing to grant they may be "right," only I hold the word "right" does not apply in matters of art, it being in the last analysis a matter of personal preference. Nothing is more futile than the attempt to reduce criticism to the level of a science.

But to those who have read little or nothing of Henry James, and among the men and women who have succeeded in reading my article up to this point, I know there are some who have not read him at all, let me make a few suggestions. Henry James is not negligible. No man of genius is negligible, and he was a man of genius. Begin by reading any of the short stories that he wrote before he was thirty, say *Travelling Companions, A Landscape Painter, The Madonna of the Future,* and it is certain that you will read more. Of the full-length novels written between 1870 and 1880, read *Roderick Hudson, The American, The Portrait of a Lady.* These are imperishable works, a glory to American literature, and in the front rank of English novels.

His masterpiece is *The American.* It is a good story well told. It is a living organism, with all the parts fitly framed together. It has a genuine plot, which develops with serene art; it is filled with living characters, that attract and repel like the persons we actually know. The form of the novel is so near perfection that I call it flawless; and I can think at this moment of only four flawless novels, Hawthorne's *Scarlet Letter,* Flaubert's *Madame Bovary,* Turgenev's *Fathers and Children,* and James's *The American.* Tolstoi's *Anna Karenina* is a greater novel than any of these, but it is not nearly so beautiful to contemplate. I mean its outline is not nearly so smooth. The four that I mentioned have, in addition to the intense interest in the story and in the characters, an outline as superb as a perfect piece of sculpture.

The American himself is a good fellow, whom every reader loves; he has conquered all obstacles hitherto, and he has every reason to believe that success will crown his efforts in what more and more takes on the aspect of the greatest adventure of his life. It is only very gradually that his confidence (and ours) is shaken, only by an accumulation of difficulties which in a cheap novel the hero would easily brush aside, that his case becomes hopeless. Readers of to-day, who are accustomed to see the American hero triumph in all his undertakings, are dismayed at the frustration of so fine and strong a man; and at the end they cannot forgive him for forgiving. But upon reflexion, taking into account all the circumstances, it is clear that no other ending was artistically, that is, truthfully, possible; one reason for the greatness of the book. I have read this story attentively three times, and I say that every time it gains in interest, and the first impression deepens.

No test is sharper than the test of rereading; what would become of most American novels published in the last few years if we read them twice? Yet as every view in nature and every good picture is surely worth a second look, so every good book is worth reading twice.

Of all the novels written by Henry James, only two called forth a general and heated discussion at the time of their appearance. Both were short, which partly accounts for their comparatively wide circle of readers. I refer to *Daisy Miller* (1878) and *The Turn of the Screw* (1898). I was a boy when Daisy was born, but I well remember the acrimonious discussions among my elders. It is a proof of the vitality of the girl Daisy Miller, that such intense interest was aroused by her fate. She is the reverse of complex; perhaps never was there a heroine so simple, so ordinary in mind, about whom such fierce discussion raged. Daisy is just a pretty girl—the average type of pretty girl—with no intellectual gifts worth mentioning, with no originality, no wit, no humour, no temperament; she says nothing interesting. After all, it is well that her creator slew her; for what place is there for Daisy in middle age, after her facial beauty has faded? Daisy Miller at forty-five is more appalling to contemplate than young Daisy in the cemetery. Yet there are few heroines whose death affects us so painfully, and the reason is that she is so absolutely *alive.*

It is possible, that Henry James, like Samuel Richardson, received many letters protesting against the fate of his heroine, insisting that she must not remain dead; for he rather contemptuously, as if to satisfy the herd, wrote and published later *Daisy Miller, A Comedy,* in which the story is retold in the form of a play, ending in the most cheerful fashion. This version appears to be not very well known; to those therefore, who cannot bear to have Daisy die, I suggest that they read this amusing comedy, where they will have the satisfaction of seeing the girl recover from the fever.

The other book, *The Turn of the Screw,* is the most nerve-shattering ghost story I have ever read, and I have read a great many. Shortly after its publication, I happened to see a copy of it on the table in the college library. I carried it home, and started reading it late at night, feeling sure that the results would be sanitary and salutary, that it would hasten the approaches of somnolence, and ensure a good night's sleep. I read it therefore totally unprepared for its unspeakable horror. For the ordinary ghost story I have little respect. Familiarity breeds contempt more with ghosts than with mortals. One must not see too many of them nor any of them too often. Furthermore, one is made callous by the machinery of melodrama. The ordinary ghost story endeavours to create an atmosphere, and usually succeeds merely in preparing the reader so that his nerves resist the attack. But here was an author who had never indulged in horrors; here was a book quite free from the witching time of night, and the scenery appropriate to the tomb. The English country-seat was charming, the weather amenable, the style of the author customarily agreeable, quiet, well-bred; but as I read on, and saw that man and then that woman, who had died and been buried, revisiting the scenes of their mortal activities, I felt an icy chill in my blood, my hair rising, my spine curling. I read on and on in horrible fascination, and when at last I finished the book, I was confronted with a terrible problem. I had to go downstairs and put out the hall light. I simply could not bear to do this, and yet, being a Yankee, I did not like to let the lower lights be burning. I could not have gone down that staircase alone; and I said to some one who stood at the top, "Don't you go away, don't you leave me for a moment! If you do, I shall never put out this light." She stood there, and kept reassuring me. Even so, I had an awful moment just after I had extinguished the gleam. No ghost story has ever affected me like that, with such veritable terror. Therefore I call it the best ghost-story I have read.

It is a profoundly moral sermon on the text in Shakespeare; the evil that men do lives after them. The lovely children have been left in the care of servants whose wickedness survived their departure, and who reach horrible hands out from the grave to destroy the boy and girl committed to their charge.

Shortly after the publication of this story, its author began the composition of another tale dealing with spirits, called *The Sense of the Past.* It is a pity that he did not live to complete it, for I think it is far and away the best novel of his later years. For some reason he had laid aside the dictated manuscript, and when the war began, he was hard at work on a novel called *The Ivory Tower,* which if complete would assuredly have been a failure. He worked at it doggedly, however, even as Stevenson worked at that inferior book, *St. Ives,* writing against the grain. Then, just as Stevenson, under inspiration, impatiently flung aside the wretched stuff, and began to write with joyous inspiration that masterpiece, *Weir of Hermiston,* which, alas! he did not live to finish, so Henry James, finding the dogs of war making such a noise that he could not go on with the trivialities of *The Ivory Tower,* bethought himself of that fragment, *The Sense of the Past,* and continued its composition with immense gusto, mounted on a flood of creative power. He redictated the pages already composed, went ahead confidently, full of vitality, knowing he was inspired. Then he was interrupted by his last illness.

Nearly four books of this novel had been finished, and in the published fragment we are acquainted with the chief characters. By a miracle, the style is transparently clear, the story progresses fast and undeviatingly, and thus, even as it stands, it must be reckoned among the masterpieces of fiction. One is conscious in reading it of the author's happy and untrammelled ease in composition.

It deals with spirits; and it is an interesting fact that in these later novels when he wrote of real people his style became obscure and hopelessly involved, and when he wrote of spooks his language cleared. His last novel is once more the international type; and among the actual persons in the story, the American Ambassador in London, presented to us with the author's whole-hearted sympathy and respect, is identified with James Russell Lowell.

It is vain to imagine what kind of style he would have employed had he lived to write more; but it is passing strange, after the difficulties that cloud and obscure the long succession of novels written in the twentieth century, that this last one of all should be written with such clarity.

From his "middle period" on, the style of Henry James became more and more difficult, so that to the majority even of intelligent readers his later books are more interesting as puzzles than as works of fiction. And when he revised his earlier novels for the New York edition, he did not improve them. Miss Clara McIntyre, of the University of Wyoming, has made a careful comparison of the old and revised versions, with the result that she has, at least to my satisfaction, proved that he would in most instances, have done better to let the books stand as they were first published. It became increasingly difficult for him to say a simple thing in a simple way. Illustrations establish her case. Take Roderick Hudson.

Original version: "Miss Stackpole's brilliant eyes expanded still farther."

Revised: "Miss Stackpole's ocular surfaces unwinkingly caught the sun."

Original version: "shaking his hunting-whip with little quick strokes."

Revised: "still agitating, in his mastered emotion, his implement of the chase."

Let me also select an instance, the death of Daisy Miller.

Original version: "But, as Winterbourne had said, it mattered very little. A week after this the poor girl died; it had been a terrible case of the fever."

Revised, "But, as Winterbourne had originally judged, the truth on this question had small actual relevance. A week after this the poor girl died; it had been indeed a terrible case of the *perniciosa.*"

If one wishes to know why the later novels lack something so gloriously and abundantly evident in the earlier, a study of the revisions that he thought improvements ought to satisfy one's curiosity. He became more and more fastidious; more and more difficult; and while it is fine to see an author struggling for perfection, I wish he had trusted his genius more and his critical talents less. He was forever after shades of meaning, and ordinary language did not express them. The failure of the later books consists really in his continual struggle to express the inexpressible. The critic finally mastered the creator. I applaud his ideals, his resolution in following them, but——

Well, let his brother speak for me. If his own brother, who was the foremost philosopher of his time, and who had spent his life investigating the most difficult of all subjects, could not understand him, if fraternal love, intimacy, sympathy, reenforcing the most highly trained mind in the world were baffled by these twentieth century novels, surely there is some excuse for me. William wrote him as follows:

> You know how opposed your whole "third manner" of execution is to the literary ideals which animate my crude and Orsonlike breast, mine being to say a thing in one sentence as straight and explicit as it can be made, and then to drop it forever; yours being to avoid naming it straight, but by dint of breathing and sighing all round and round it, to arouse in the reader who may have had a similar perception already (heaven help him if he hasn't!) the illusion of a solid object, made . . . wholly out of impalpable materials, air and the prismatic interferences of light, ingeniously focused by mirrors upon empty space. But you do it, that's the queerness! . . . But it's the rummest method for one to employ systematically as you do

nowadays; and you employ it at your peril. . . . You can't skip a word if you are to get the effect, and nineteen out of twenty worthy readers grow intolerant. The method seems perverse. "Say it out, for God's sake," they cry, "and have done with it." And so I say now, give us one thing in your older, directer manner, just to show that, in spite of your paradoxical success in this unheard-of method, you can still write according to accepted canons. Give us that interlude; and then continue like the "curiosity of literature" which you have become. For gleams and innuendos and felicitous verbal insinuations you are unapproachable, but the core of literature is solid.

The spectacle of a professional metaphysician on his knees to a novelist, begging him to write intelligently, has a humour all its own. William was undoubtedly right. Henry in his later novels is unnecessarily obscure, as were George Meredith,. Robert Browning, Maurice Maeterlinck, and Henrik Ibsen in certain portions—not the best portions—of their productions. In his *Recollections* Lord Morley, in speaking of George Meredith, said that we cannot accept a writer's protestations that he is not obscure if the majority of his readers insist that they cannot understand him. We might just as well be in a dark room and pretend to believe one man who protests that the room has abundance of light. We know better. Just as no man can possibly be the final judge of his own worth, so no man can determine finally whether what he says is or is not obscure.

There is a sentence in *The Sacred Fount* (1901) that often rises in my mind when I am reading James: "How can I tell, please, what you consider you're talking about?" And we often feel as though we were maddeningly close to the idea without quite perceiving it, which is unconsciously expressed for us by another sentence in the same novel. "It affected me again that she could get so near without getting nearer." But the best sentence in the same book expresses not only the highest happiness that our author found in life, but something of our own pleasure in his best work.

For real excitement there are no such adventures as intellectual ones. This is why he went on writing in his own manner, despite the loss of popularity and the frenzied pleadings of his brother. For, notwithstanding the mental torture caused by the study of *The Golden Bowl* and of *The Ambassadors,* we know well enough they are works of genius. Their greatness is as clear as their meaning is dark. Part of their obscurity arises from the fact that the author was exploring the dimmest regions of human thought, the last complexity of mixed motives, the blackest hour before the real dawn of passion. It is easier for a popular novelist to be clear than it was for James; it was easier for Pope to be clear than it was for Browning.

Analysis is the key-word. *Daisy Miller* is called neither a novel nor a story. It is called a "study." And it is just as much a study as a doctor's thesis. So is *In the Cage, The Turn of the Screw, The Princess Casamassima, What Maisie Knew,* and all the rest. In the earlier novels, there was plenty of analysis, but synthesis finally triumphed, as it should in every completed work of art; the whole was greater than the sum of its parts. In the later novels, analysis reigned supreme. The attempt, if there were one, to summarise, failed; and while we are lost in admiration of individual scenes and sentences—(the opening of *The Golden Bowl* is perfect)—at the very last we grasp vainly at shadows.

No other American novelist has had a more powerful influence on true craftsmen than Henry James, and this fact is more apparent every day. He has three disciples of whom any man might be proud—Joseph Conrad, Edith Wharton, Anne Sedgwick. All three are original writers, but all three have been powerfully affected by the work of James, and all three are glad to acknowledge it. Hosts of lesser-known men and women in the third decade of our amazing century are trying to write like him; in most cases they fail because they have nothing to say.

His secret was his own, because he was a man of genius. In attempting to describe his later style I have made the phrase "verbose reticence," which seems to me to express his manner and his mannerisms. No writer has ever used more words to describe a shade of feeling, a penumbra of recollection; yet after penetrating through circle after circle of phrases, the final truth is wrapped in mystery. He was enormously voluminous and extraordinarily reticent.

In addition to his mastery of the art of the novel and of the short story, I am inclined to believe that he was the greatest literary critic ever born in America. He produced a number of critical works that display insight; and his book, modestly called *Notes on Novelists* (1914), is the most illuminating criticism of the Continental and English novel that I have seen. Nor has any one come nearer than he to saying the final word on the much-discussed question of the place of sex in fiction. He believed in the traditional Anglo-Saxon and American reserve and reverence, remarking that in the case of those writers who loudly insist that sex must have its "place" in novels, there very soon appears to be no place for anything else.

When this book appeared, I could not help writing him my appreciation, asking him at the same time not to think of acknowledging it. But the following letter came speedily, and I quote it here because it shows the generous, affectionate nature of the man, the terrible cloud of oppression over his spirit during the war, and yet how much honest and sincere praise pleased him; it shows that no matter how austere he was as a professional artist, he was in all human relations simple, natural, and lovable.

December 15th, 1914.
21, Carlyle Mansions,
Cheyne Walk. S. W.

DEAR W. L. PHELPS:

But I *must* thank you for the pleasure given me by your generous lines about my "Notes"—letting you measure what that is by the fact that under this huge nightmare, the unprecedented oppression or obsession of our public consciousness here, pleasure (save of the grim sort that premonitions of Victory, terrifically paid for, bring) is very hard to take and very questionable even to desire. However, I rejoice without scruple in what you tell me of your so liberal appreciation of my book—and if I could only have been present in time—and in spirit—at your expounding lecture (it would have helped things even for your author), this would have represented, oh, such a blest break in the constant comprehensive ache of yours all faithfully

HENRY JAMES.

HOWELLS

Ah, poor Real Life, which I love, can I make others see the delight I find in thy foolish and insipid face?

The literary career of Mr. Howells covered exactly sixty years, his first book appearing in 1860. His published works number more than one hundred; they form a complete library. They include novels, poems, plays, literary essays, short stories, sketches of travel, autobiography and spiritual confessions. Despite the enormous quantity of his production, his composition shows no evidence of haste. He seemed to write evenly and tranquilly, with a style accurately fitted to the subject. His friend Henry James, whose every word was an awarded prize out of a host of competitors, never ceased to wonder at the excellent quality of this inexhaustible flow.

WILLIAM DEAN HOWELLS

I should think it would make you as happy as poor happiness will let us be, to turn off from one year to the other, and from a reservoir in daily, domestic use, such a free, full, rich flood. In fact your reservoir deluges me, altogether, with surprise as well as other sorts of effusion; by which I mean that though you do much to empty it you keep it remarkably full. I seem to myself, in comparison, to fill mine with a teaspoon and obtain but a trickle. However, I don't mean to compare myself with you or to compare you, in the particular case, with anything but life. When I do that—with the life you see and represent—your faculty for representing it seems to me extraordinary—and to shave the truth—the general truth you aim at—several degrees closer than anyone else begins to do. You are less *big* than Zola, but you are ever so much less clumsy and more really various, and moreover you and he don't see the same things—you have a wholly different consciousness—*you* see a wholly different side of a different race. Man isn't at all *one,* after all—it takes so much of him to be American, to be French, etc. I won't even compare you with something I have a sort of dim stupid sense you might be and are not—for I don't in the least know that you might be it, after all, or whether, if you were, you wouldn't cease to be that something you are which makes me write to you thus. We don't know what people might give us that they don't—the only thing is to take them on what they do and to allow them absolutely and utterly their conditions . . . the fact there's a whole quarter of the heavens upon which, in the matter of composition, you seem consciously—*is* it consciously?—to have turned your back; but these things have no relevancy whatever as grounds of dislike—simply because you communicate so completely *what* you undertake to communicate. The novelist is a particular *window*, absolutely—and of worth so far as he is one; and it's because you open so well and are hung so close over the street that I could hang out of it all day long.

Omitting men whose art is identified with the short story, America has produced five novelists of international distinction—Cooper, Hawthorne, Mark Twain, Henry James, and Howells. It is interesting to observe that not one of these bears any true resemblance to the other four. One might expect in a "new" country, necessarily influenced by the precepts and models of older nations, characterised by the timidity that invariably accompanies lack of self-assurance, that our leading novelists would show unmistakable family likeness. The exact opposite is the truth. It has been asserted that the younger British novelists of to-day are so similar that it would be easy to mistake the product of one for that of another; whether this be true or not—and I am by no means sure of it—imagine Cooper scribbling *The Marble Faun,* Mark Twain signing the last page of *Deerslayer,* Hawthorne composing *Their Wedding Journey,* Howells writing *The Golden Bowl,* and Henry James dictating *Huckleberry Finn!*

Apart from the inevitable inspiration given to one writer by another, our American quincunx remains a fixed pattern. Each individual would have been much the same if the others had never existed. The influences in evidence were indeed more repellant than otherwise. Howells never fully appreciated Hawthorne; Henry James was rather contemptuous towards Mark Twain; while Mark Twain threw everything he could reach at Cooper. Cooper was not witty in himself, but he was the cause of wit in other men.

We Americans have reason to be proud of our famous Five. Each made a distinct contribution to literature. Cooper was a pioneer in romances of woods and waves, and was one of the greatest novelists of action in literary history; Hawthorne, in his own sphere of imaginative realism, has never been surpassed; as a purely psychological realist, with the emphasis on the adjective, Henry

James is unique; Howells made correct portraits of American city and country life; whilst Mark Twain himself answered the query which had become almost petulant by repetition, "Who will write the great American novel?" For *Huckleberry Finn* is not only the great American novel; it is America.

It is as a novelist that Howells will be remembered. He set up a department-store of literature, where the visitor could buy anything from a song to a sermon; but much of the stock remains on the shelves. I have never met anybody who could quote a line of his poetry; and his essays in literary criticism are perishable freight. His criticism is valuable for the revelation of his own temperament, for its shrewd observations on life in general, for its delicate humour; but he never had the truly critical mind. He seemed to me to betray this fact—quite unconsciously, of course—in one of the conversations it was my privilege to have with him. "I am tempted to make a resolution never to write another word of literary criticism. When I write any critical judgment, it seems to me to be wholly, definitely true; I cannot for the life of me see how anybody else can hold a different opinion. Then some days or months later, I experience a disagreeable shock; for I discover that some other person contradicts everything I have said." He spoke these words with no trace of humour, no mock dismay; they were uttered seriously, with charming candour. I confess I was amazed. No matter how strong one's convictions may be or how tenaciously held, it seems to me that the first requisite of criticism should be the ability to understand how a person of at least equal intelligence and probity should support precisely opposite opinions with equal ardour. President Roosevelt and President Wilson were not meant to be literary critics, for they seemed amusingly alike in honestly thinking that those who disagreed with them lacked both intelligence and morality.

Mr. Howell's belief in realism amounted almost to a religion. He felt that art, like human intercourse, should be founded on literal truth. To him all romanticists were liars. In the year 1911 he reviewed his own critical work in *Harper's Magazine* as follows: "From the first it was a polemic, a battle. I detested the sentimental and the romantic in fiction, and I began at once to free my mind concerning the romanticists, as well dead as alive. (Note the delightful ambiguity of the last five words.) As I could not in conscience spare either age or sex the effect of my reasons, I soon had every lover of romanticism hating me and saying I had said worse things about it than I had ever said, whatever I had thought. In fact, I carefully kept myself from personalities; but that did not save me from them either on this shore of the sea or the other. I remember one English reviewer beginning a notice of my book of Criticism and Fiction, which grew out of The Study essays, by saying 'This man has placed himself beyond the pale of decency,' and then, in proof, going on to behave indecently towards me. . . . When after six years' warfare I gave up writing The Study . . . I owned it had been a rigourous experience. . . . The worst of it I did not then perceive, or know that my long fight had been a losing fight; I perceive now that the monstrous rag baby of romanticism is as firmly in the saddle as it was before the joust began, and that it always will be, as long as the children of men are childish."

Such a confession is both honest and charming; but it is a proof of the absence of the critical temper. Every critic should have a hospitable mind, even if all his criticism be written from one standpoint. Mr. Howells simply showed the door to romanticists; whereas a realistic work, although it violated his habit of reserve, was greeted with enthusiasm. His public reception of *Jude the Obscure* was almost obstreperous in its heartiness; yet I believe he would have died rather than have written such a book.

Although the novels of Mr. Howells are for the most part rigourously objective, one cannot fail to obtain through them some notion of their author's temperament and character. Gerhart Hauptmann says, "An artist will not put his opinions and his beliefs into his dramas and stories; but any intelligent person, after reading a considerable number of them, ought to be able to discover what kind of a man wrote them." The superstructure of our novelist's education was so different from its foundation that the combination is plainly seen in his life, his character, and his written work. Ohio plus Italy—subterranean solidity supporting beauty and grace. Brought up by simple, sincere, God-fearing parents, spending the years of boyhood setting type and writing articles in a Middle West country newspaper office, he was made United States Consul at Venice at the age of twenty-four. Imagine the effect of a residence in Italy on the mind and temperament of an Ohio youth, who had already published a volume of poems! His sensitiveness to Venetian impressions was quickened by the romance of love, for at twenty-five he was married; his marriage exhibiting the same combination of rural America with a Continental city, for he was married in Paris, and his bride came from Vermont.

Mr. Howells wrote many books on foreign scenes, and became in every sense a citizen of the world, but he never lost the simplicity, democracy, and honesty that characterised his father's household. Just as Abraham Lincoln was always and everywhere the same man, whether in a country lawyer's office or receiving a delegation of diplomats in the White House, so Mr. Howells, whether in

Boston, New York, or London, always exhaled something of the Middle West. He was a chameleon only artistically and histrionically—the moment one talked with him alone, one felt an unadorned Americanism as sturdy as it was unaggressive. Good home training is always worth more than school or college, and it left an indelible stamp on our novelist. To his last days, the spirit of his parents talked through his lips, and held the pen while he wrote.

For all of which, I, for one, am devoutly thankful. He was, in influence, as well as in name, a Dean. For many years he was looked up to as the first of our living writers of fiction, and he had more effect on the tone, quality, and tendencies of American novels than any other person. From the earliest story of Mary Wilkins to the latest tale by Zona Gale, Mr. Howells is somewhere in evidence. His two great rivals, Mark Twain and Henry James, could not possibly throw the breadth of literary influence extended by him; for Mark Twain had the uniqueness that sometimes, though not always, accompanies genius, and Henry James, unfortunately for the world, has never been read except by a few. His influence is deep rather than wide; it is seen in individuals.

Many rebellions were organised against the domination of Mr. Howells; but they sputtered out. One reason for their futility was the fact that those who tried to break the chains of what they called his tyranny were themselves conspicuously feeble; for, quarrel with his reticences and his superficialities as we may, from the very start he possessed the secret of style. He seems always to have known how to write—a fundamental thing in literary art, though contemporary poets and novelists may not all think so.

Even his chronicles of very small beer—*Annie Kilburn* for example—are exquisitely done. It is easy apparently for his adverse critics to make the mistake of identifying his creations with himself—of supposing, because he deliberately chose to write of commonplace characters and trivial incidents, that therefore he himself was trivial and commonplace. But it was quite otherwise. His hatred of melodrama and sentimentality made him select those aspects of life which are samples, where people of average intelligence, average character, average income, pass through average experiences. He was a skilful player without any trumps. What would some of our successful shockers do with the cards he drew from the pack?

He chose to portray real life as he knew it by observation and experience. He was a Realist by instinct and by training. He was so kindly that no one thinks of him as a good hater; but he had, after all, an average human capacity for hatred, and the two things in the world he hated most were falsehood and affectation. The word *Snob* made him see red. It is curious to see how the natural honesty of the man affected his own creative fiction and limited his sympathies as a critic. In him we find something by no means universal—a union of moral passion with the artistic temperament. He disliked any person or any book that did not ring true; he hated snobs and snobbery because they illustrated the vice of affectation, and in talking about such things he was as violent as he knew how to be.

It was, I think, merely his love of truth that made him write stories where every page could be verified, and made him unsympathetic to books of romance. He was right in despising many of the pseudo-historical romances with which America was flooded during the last decade of the last century; he lumped all these together as "romantic rot," and I have seen him laugh till the tears came while quoting specimens of their anachronistic oaths and bogus jargon. When I called his attention to the chronically gymnastic heroines who were always drawing themselves up to their full height, I feared for his health.

Those were bad days for the root-and-branch realists, because, owing to the influence of Stevenson and the reaction against the excesses of realism, the public had suddenly gone mad over romance. It is interesting to look back and see how that outbreak in the 'nineties affected our American triumviate—Howells, Henry James, and Mark Twain. No really important novel came from the first, though he resolutely refused to compromise; Henry James spent six years in a futile endeavour to write a successful play, and then, in 1898, wrote a dramatic ghost story, *The Turn of the Screw;* Mark

Twain launched a romantic dreadnought called *Joan of Arc.*

If anyone had suggested to Mr. Howells that the philosophy of romance postulated the *summum bonum* as Beauty, regardless of whether or not it had any relation to Truth, he would probably have responded that to his mind everything was ugly that was not true.

It is fortunate for Americans that our leading novelists—Hawthorne, Mark Twain, Henry James, and Howells—all wrote guide-books to the European scene. For a summer tour on the Continent, or for a prolonged sojourn, no better travelling companions can be found than these four. I do not think anyone has ever written a more vivid description of the beautiful tower in Siena than Mr. Howells:

> It was in the clearness that follows the twilight when, after the sudden descent of a vaulted passage, I stood in the piazza and saw the Tower of the Mangia leap like a rocket into the starlit air. After all, that does not say it; you must suppose a perfect silence, through which this exquisite shaft forever soars. When once you have seen the Mangia, all other towers, obelisks, and columns are tame and vulgar and earth-rooted; *that* seems to

quit the ground, to be not a monument but a flight. The crescent of the young moon . . . looked sparely over the battlements of the Palazzo Communale, from which the tower sprang, upon the fronts of the beautiful old palaces . . . and touched with silver the waters of the loveliest fountain in the world.

Although he was twenty-three when his volume of poems was published, his first novel did not appear until he had reached the age of thirty-four. During the intervening eleven years he was storing observations and impressions of Italy and Europe, and by constant practice had obtained a command of the art of writing English prose, proved in four separate publications, dealing with foreign travel and suburban sketches at home. His first novel and the two that shortly followed it were satisfying evidence that a new master of the art of fiction had appeared in America. These three books, *Their Wedding Journey, A Chance Acquaintance, A Foregone Conclusion,* exhibit a variety of qualities that unite in a general effect of charm. Real characters, steadily if slowly advancing narrative, brilliant dialogue, salted with genuine humour—these are the invariable features of Mr. Howells's early stories.

Before their appearance in book form, the three novels had been printed in *The Atlantic Monthly,* as indeed were not a few of their successors; and it was during Mr. Howells's service on the editorial staff of this magazine that he was able to assist a man who was to be his life-long friend and rival—Henry James. The younger man was not "discovered" by the elder, as has often been stated, but substantial help towards recognition was given, a favour never forgotten by the recipient. In the year 1866, shortly after his return from Italy, Mr. Howells was invited by Mr. Fields to become assistant editor of *The Atlantic Monthly.* Five years later he took the post of editor, his connexion with the magazine covering fifteen years, during which time he not only passed judgment on manuscripts submitted, but wrote an immense amount himself. It was in this very year 1866, that Henry James, then twenty-three years old, sent in a contribution called *Poor Richard.* Mr. Fields handed it to the assistant editor, with the question, "Shall we accept it?" Mr. Howells read it, and immediately replied, "Yes, and all the stories you can get from that writer." This episode led to an intimacy between the two Americans, one twenty-nine, the other twenty-three, which existed without a shadow for fifty years. Mr. Albert Mordell does not exaggerate when he calls it "one of the great literary friendships in the annals of literature."

The difference characterising the aims of the two men is apparent in their earliest work; even as a boy, Henry James was a meditative, speculative student, much given to analysis, and he remained just that to his last day. While James was "studying," Howells was reporting for a newspaper, and a reporter of life he was to the end. I cannot help thinking that the journalistic work on that Ohio newspaper affected the novelist's art in no small degree. It made him observant rather than introspective, a chronicler rather than an analyser of life. He never lost zest for minute observation; nothing characteristically human seemed dull or unimportant. His eye was microscopic, and when he turned it on what some call commonplace events or commonplace people, they swarmed with exciting activities, as any tiny bit of life does under a microscope. "We had no idea it was so interesting!"

The novels of his first decade—the 'seventies—reached a climax in *The Lady of the Aroostook,* published in 1879. I remember the delight with which I read this new book. To those who have forgotten it I can still heartily recommend taking the voyage to Europe with Lydia, and seeing Italy with her clear, virginal vision. The contrast between her rural home in New England and her Italian environment makes for a pure type of high comedy. Mr. Howells is one of that small minority who can see fellow countrymen and women travelling about Europe, without hating them. I do not know why it should be so; but men of all nations who have been "abroad" seem to find their fellow citizens in foreign scenes unendurable. Is this a pose? Is it an assumption of superior knowledge? At all events, the travelling American cannot be nearly so odious to the natives as he is to men and women of his own land. Do they resent his intrusion? What is the reason for this contemptuous hostility? Observe how those who have remained for some time in an expensive hotel stare at newcomers. But Mr. Howells seemed to love his raw countrymen even in sacred European surroundings.

Unquestionably, the best part of his career was the decade between 1880 and 1890, for, although he was to write steadily for thirty years after the close of this period, he never, with one exception, came near the heights again. As has happened so frequently with other creative artists, he produced in rapid succession works that constitute his surest claim on the future. He was in the vein, and must have known it. In a short space of time, he published *A Modern Instance, The Rise of Silas Lapham, Indian Summer,* and *A Hazard of New Fortunes*—books too familiar to need any particular comment here, except to remark that the first two of the quartette are perhaps the most purely American of all his productions; *Indian Summer* reveals the charm of the city of Florence so poignantly that it makes one homesick for the Arno; *A Hazard of New Fortunes* exhibits that dawning interest in sociological problems, which, together with the influence of Tolstoi, was to affect his work not wholly beneficially for the rest of his life. Although *The Rise of Silas Lapham* is almost universally regarded as his masterpiece, I think it inferior to *A Modern Instance*—the most tragic, the most powerful, the most deep-rooted of all his novels.

In 1890 appeared a delightful bit of autobiography, called *A Boy's Town,* written for *Harper's Young People.* Then for thirty years came a steady succession of novels, plays, works of criticism, autobiographical writings, none of which is without value, but all—with one exception—making no real ad dition to his fame. For nearly fifteen years the younger generation forsook his precepts and wandered after what he believed to be false gods. It is pleasant to remember that his reputation was higher in 1920 than in 1900.

The exception is the novel called *The Kentons,* published in 1902. As I am afraid that this book is not nearly so widely read as it deserves to be, and as I am certain that nine out of ten readers will share my enthusiasm for it, I wish to say emphatically that it is one of the finest works of fiction Mr. Howells ever composed; it reveals all the qualities that made his reputation in the 'eighties, mellowed and sweetened by age. It is the chronicle of an absolutely representative Ohio family, who are driven to spending a winter in New York, and are then forced into the hazardous experiment of a European journey. Every character in this story is a triumph of creation; they are so real that they leave the reader in a glow of enthusiastic recognition. On finishing the book, I could not help writing to its author, and his reply, dated 24 July 1902, may be as interesting to others as to the recipient. "Your letter gave me so much joy. . . . You have touched my heart with your praise of Ellen Kenton; and Boyne *is* good, I won't deny it."

Now, on the matter of *The Kentons,* I am absolutely firm in the faith; I know it is first-rate work. But eighteen years had passed since its appearance, and I feared I was the only man in the world (except its author) who knew how good it was, for it is a book seldom mentioned. And so when I read the *Letters* of Henry James, which abound in self-revelation and keen criticism,

I could not repress an ejaculation in finding a letter written to Mr. Howells on 12 September 1902, which expresses unlimited enthusiasm over this same novel: ". . . that I should have joyed so in 'The Kentons,' which you sent me, ever so kindly, more weeks ago than it would be decent in me to count—should have eaten and drunk and dreamed and thought of them as I did, should have sunk into them, in short, so that they closed over my head like living waters and kept me down, down in subaqueous prostration . . . : there was a time when I talked of nothing and nobody else, and I have scarcely even now come to the end of it. I think in fact it is *because* I have been so busy vaunting and proclaiming them, up and down the more or less populated avenues of my life, that I have had no time left for anything else. . . . The impression of the book remains, and I have infinitely pleased myself even in my shame, with thinking of the pleasure that must have come to yourself from so acclaimed and attested a demonstration of the freshness, within you still, of the spirit of evocation. Delightful, in one's golden afternoon, and after many days and many parturitions, to put forth thus a young, strong, living flower. You have done nothing more true and complete, more thoroughly homogeneous and hanging-together, without the faintest ghost of a false note or a weak touch—all as sharply ciphered-up and tapped out as the 'proof' of a prize scholar's sum on a slate. It is in short miraculously felt and beautifully done, and the aged—by which I mean the richly-matured—sposi *as* done as if sposi were a new and fresh idea to you. Of all your sposi they are, I think, the most penetrated and most penetrating. I took in short true comfort in the whole manifestation, the only bitterness in the cup being that it made me feel old. I shall never again so renew myself."

The noticeable reticence in the art of Mr. Howells—which led him instinctively to shun detailed descriptions of the coarser aspects of life—sprang, I think, from a certain delicacy in his nature so remarkable that I have never seen its like in any other man. It is astonishing that one who was brought up in a newspaper office, who was at home in every city of the world, who must have met all varieties of human nature, should have remained so virginally sensitive. He never used bad language—he did not like to see it in print; he not only never smoked, the odour of tobacco in a room was almost intolerable to him (which shows how he must have loved his friend); and there is a curious statement in his article on Mark Twain, which is truly revealing. He said that in spite of Mark Twain's boisterous humour and profanity, there was an innate gentleness and refinement in him; *he never put his hands on you.* Evidently the friendly arm on the shoulder, the added emphasis of touch, was something horrible to Mr. Howells, and when I read that sentence, I wondered if, in the many conversations I had enjoyed with him, I had ever tortured him in that way. That is a curious aversion, most unusual; for Henry James, who seemed as an author so fastidious and distant, would put his arm affectionately around your neck at the first interview. These things are worth recording, for they help to explain the silences in his books. Yet Mr. Howells was the last man in the world that I should call effeminate. He was so masculine, so democratic, so simple, that I shall always think of him as a homespun American.

No tribute to his art would be complete without a tribute to the beauty of his character. I never met a better man than Mr. Howells, I never saw one who was more generous, more sincere, more genuine, more essentially noble.

From a steel engraving by J. A. J. Wilcox, after a photograph.
Reproduced by permission of Houghton Mifflin Company.

HARRIET BEECHER STOWE

UNCLE TOM'S CABIN

Although it is rather the fashion to call American Literature second rate, some of it has enjoyed a world-wide popularity, and exerted a universal influence. Benjamin Franklin, Fenimore Cooper, Edgar Allan Poe, H. W. Longfellow, R. W. Emerson, Walt Whitman, Nathaniel Hawthorne, Joel Chandler Harris, Mark Twain, are known and read in most European and some Asiatic languages. In addition to books by these men, there is one American novel that continues to have a steady sale and is read every year in the uttermost parts of the earth. Although *Uncle Tom's Cabin* was written as propaganda, it has long survived the institution it attacked, and it is probable that future generations will regard it as a prime favourite. What is the cause of the seemingly eternal vitality of this story?

Harriet Beecher was born at Litchfield, Conn., 14 June 1811. Her father, the Rev. Lyman Beecher, was a distinguished man, and would conceivably be more famous to-day if he had not been overshadowed by his daughter the novelist, and by his son Henry Ward Beecher. When she was twenty-one, her father moved to Cincinnati. There she, with her sister, started a school for girls. In Cincinnati her father was President of a Theological Seminary; and in 1836, Harriet was married to Calvin Stowe, a professor in the institution. They lived in Cincinnati till 1850. Her life was a chronic fight against poverty and sickness, with the importunate problem of bringing up a family on a microscopic income. She did much hackwork. She wrote articles for newspapers, and small magazines; she published a geography; she worked day and night.

Ohio was a border-state, where she saw continually one aspect of the slavery question. Her father and her husband were strong anti-slavery men, and the daily family conversation was largely devoted to passionate discussions. The house was a refuge for runaway slaves; and some that had been freed became in a way members of the family.

"I was a child in 1820," she once wrote, "when the Missouri question was agitated, and one of the strongest and deepest impressions on my mind was that made by my father's sermons and prayers, and the anguish of his soul for the poor slave at that time. I remember his preaching drawing tears down the hardest faces of the old farmers in his congregation. I well remember his prayers morning and evening in the family for 'poor, oppressed, bleeding Africa,' that the time of her deliverance might come; prayers offered with strong crying and tears which indelibly impressed my heart and made me what I am from my very soul, the enemy of all slavery. Every brother I have has been in his sphere a leading anti-slavery man. As for myself and husband, we have for the last seventeen years lived on the border of a slave State, and we have never shrunk from the fugitives, and we have helped them with all we had to give. I have received the children of liberated slaves into a family school, and taught them with my own children, and it has been the influence that we found in the church and by the altar that has made us do all this."

In 1850, her husband became a professor in Bowdoin College, Maine, which had previously given to American Literature Hawthorne and Longfellow, and was soon to see one of its alumni President of the United States. In the year of their arrival the Fugitive Slave Law brought the topic of slavery to the boiling point. A member of the family wrote to her: "If I could use a pen as you can, I would write something that would make this whole nation feel what an accursed thing slavery is." This letter excited Mrs. Stowe, and after reading it aloud, she said, "I will write something. I will if I live."

Her son tells the famous story of the conception of Uncle Tom.

"It was in the month of February (1851) that Mrs. Stowe was seated at communion service in the college church at Brunswick. Suddenly, like the unrolling of a picture, the scene of the death of Uncle Tom passed before her mind. So strongly was she affected that it was with difficulty she could keep from weeping aloud. Immediately on returning home she took pen and paper and wrote out the vision which had been, as it were, blown into her mind as by the rushing of a mighty wind. Gathering her family about her she read what she had written. Her two little sons of ten and twelve years of age broke into convulsive weeping, one of them saying through his sobs, 'Oh, Mamma! slavery is the most cruel thing in the world.' Thus Uncle Tom was ushered into the world, and it was, as we said at the beginning, a cry, an immediate, an involuntary expression of deep, impassioned feeling. Twenty-five years afterwards Mrs. Stowe wrote a letter to one of her children, of this period of her life: 'I well remember the winter you were a baby and I was writing *Uncle Tom's Cabin.* My heart was bursting with the anguish excited by the cruelty and injustice our nation was showing to the slave, and praying God to let me do a little, and to cause my cry to be heard. I remember many a night weeping over you as you lay sleeping beside me, and I thought of the slave mothers whose babes were torn from them.' "

A weekly journal called *The National Era,* devoted to the campaign against slavery, whose editor was a personal friend of Mrs.

Stowe, was being printed at Washington. Whittier had contributed poems to its pages. As fast as she wrote the manuscript, Mrs. Stowe sent thither the sheets, and *Uncle Tom's Cabin* thus appeared in installments in 1851-52. Like many another famous novel, it attracted eager and general attention during its progress in the periodical, and it was published in book form before the serial was concluded. Within four months Mrs. Stowe was paid ten thousand dollars. In an age before the era of best sellers, her novel sold over 300,000 copies the first year. Mrs. Stowe travelled in Europe, and was received everywhere as a famous author; she visited the Brownings in Italy. On her return, her husband became professor in Andover Theological Seminary, where the students called their house Uncle Tom's Cabin. In 1863 they took up their permanent residence in Hartford, where she died 1 July 1896, at the age of 85. After the war, she spent many winters in Florida, living in the South for the first time.

In an interview with Mr. Alba Honeywell, published in the Springfield *Republican* in December 1914, the vigourous man, aged 93, holding in his hand a copy of the first edition of the book, gave his visitor the following information: "I sold the first published copy of this book. Some of the folks have been making quite a fuss about it of late. I was then on the editorial staff of the *Standard* in New York City. This, you remember, was the organ of the American anti-slavery society and the official publication of the liberal party, as the abolitionists were known. *Uncle Tom's Cabin* had been published serially in the National Era at Washington in 1851 and 1852, attracting wide attention. It was brought out in book form by John P. Jewett & Co., Boston publishers, in the latter part of 1852. The very first installment which came from their press was shipped to the *Standard* office and I happened to be standing by when the consignment was opened. A gentleman whose sympathies were strongly against slavery had been haunting the office for several days waiting to buy the first copy. I picked one out of the lot and sold it to him."

This novel has never known a period of neglect. Shortly before the author's death, the publishers got out a new edition of 100,-

000 copies, which were sold in a few weeks. By 1878 it had been translated into twenty languages Shortly after the book first appeared, it was dramatised; for seventy years it has held the stage with no sign of diminishing popularity, and it is perhaps the favourite American play. It would be difficult to say how many companies are acting it at this moment, but there are many. (The name of the original adapter is George L. Aiken, and those who are interested in the origin and text of the dramatic version may be referred to the work by Montrose J. Moses, *Representative Plays by American Dramatists.*)

Like Barnum's circus, the advent of this play to a one-night stand is preceded by a morning parade, which whets the curiosity of the crowd. In the South, it means a general holiday. A northern tourist a few years ago, after ringing in vain for the bell-boy, in the hotel, asked the clerk what was the matter, and was told, "You are not acquainted with the South, sir. When I said *Uncle Tom's Cabin* was in town, that was sufficient explanation as to the whereabouts of every coloured man, woman and child for ten miles around. They are all packed out on Main

Street to see the big parade, and you couldn't get one of them to work until it passes if you gave them a dollar for each minute. If it doesn't pass pretty soon you will go without your dinner, for every cook and waiter is outside, watching for the first band. Order them to work? Well, I guess not. It would start a riot, and every one from the dish-washer to the head waiter would walk out on us and we'd be boycotted." The tourist found the streets jammed and the trees and telegraph posts crowded with pickaninnies. When Little Eva appeared, the mammies cried, "Dah now! Ah could kiss dat child to deff." Little Eva was chewing gum.

The last time I saw the play was in a New England town. At the death of Little Eva, half the audience were in tears, while the rest were laughing. Those who came to weep, did so in the rainiest fashion; those who came to scoff remained for the same purpose, and thus got their money's worth. It is a national institution. The late Hopkinson Smith declared that it should be suppressed, but the people love it too well to part with it, and the national common sense and good humour can be relied on to receive it in the proper spirit.

Uncle Tom's Cabin was more effective in arousing anti-slavery sentiment than the works of Garrison, Phillips, Whittier, Lowell, than all the congressmen and all the tracts. It was concrete. It had the eternal advantage of a story over an essay or an oration. It did not talk about the condition of the African race; it gave the world living persons. It appealed to the heart rather than to the head, to sentiment rather than reason. Everyone knows that although human beings have the capacity to reason, they seldom use it. The road to influence is through the feelings; and in times of great national crises, reason and judgment are abandoned. Furthermore, the novel directed its attack against the weakest point in the defence of slavery, and the worst abuse of the system—the breaking up of negro families by sale.

The adverse feeling aroused in the South is shown in the contemporary periodicals in that quarter, many of which were quoted in an interesting article published in *The Bookman* in 1903, by Arthur Bartlett Maurice, from which my citations are made. It is well known that in response to the attacks upon the veracity of the book, Mrs. Stowe published a key. This brought down a general castigation from the *Southern Literary Messcnger,* June 1853, in which Mrs. Stowe is not only condemned as a disseminator of incendiary falsehoods, but as an immoral writer. What would the reviewer have thought could he have foreseen the novels published in the twentieth century by "female pens"?

> It is a horrible thought that a woman should write, or a lady read such productions as those by which a celebrity has been acquired. Are scenes of license and impurity, and ideas of loathesome depravity and habitual prostitution to be made the cherished topics of the female pen, and the familiar staple of domestic consideration for promiscuous conversation? Is the mind of woman to be tainted, seduced, contaminated, and her heart disenchanted of its native purity of sentiment by the unblushing perusal, the free discussion and the frequent imitation of such thinly veiled pictures of corruption? It is sufficiently disgraceful that a woman should be the instrument of disseminating the vile stream of contagion, but it is intolerable that Southern women should defile themselves by bringing the putrid waters to their lips.

The *New Orleans Weekly Picayune,* 30 August 1852, "viewed with alarm" the proposed dramatisation of the story:

It is stated in Eastern papers that an experienced writer in Boston is engaged in dramatising the abolition novel, *Uncle Tom's Cabin.* The gross misrepresentations of the South which have been propagated so extensively through the press with the laudations of editors, politicians and pious fanatics of the pulpit, are to be presented in tableaux, and the lies they contain acted by living libellers before crowds of deluded spectators. The stage is to be employed in depicting to the people of the North the whole body of the people of the South living in a state of profligacy, cruelty and crime, tyrants who fear not God and cruelly oppress their fellow-creatures, and the drama is thus enlisted among the promoters of sectional hatred, a teacher and preacher of national discord, whose end inevitably would be the disruption of the Union.

The *Southern Quarterly Review,* January 1853, condemned the book in terms that do not need to be modified today, for they are well within the truth.

To disprove slanders thus impudently uttered and obstinately persevered in is impossible unless those who are to judge the question had some little insight into the facts of the case, and could know something of our habits and our laws, thus being enabled to judge of the respective worth of the testimony brought before them. So far from this being the case in the present question, not only is our cause prejudged, but our very accusers assume to be our judges. . . . To such as are willing to hear both sides we have endeavoured to invalidate Mrs. Stowe's testimony by proving that so far from being well acquainted with our habits and manners she has probably never set foot in our country, and is ignorant alike of our manners, feelings, and even habits of language. She makes her Southern ladies and gentlemen talk in rather vulgar Yankee-English, her Louisiana negroes all talk "Kentuck."

Mr. Maurice's valuable article, which is a contribution to the history of critical opinion, gives extensive quotations from Northern book-reviews, not all of which were favourable, and from newspapers and magazines in England. It is clear from a perusal of these that the whole world was talking about *Uncle Tom's Cabin,* and that its literary impression abroad was as wide if not as deep as its moral effect at home. It is interesting to observe that Garrison's anti-slavery paper, *The Liberator,* was cold and almost hostile to Mrs. Stowe's novel. Was he jealous? Reformers have seldom been good at co-operation.

Finally, to take one more bit from Mr. Maurice, the large number of foreign translations was playfully alluded to by Oliver

Wendell Holmes in a poem he wrote for the author's seventieth birthday:

If every tongue that speaks her praise,
For whom I shape my tinkling phrase,
  Were summoned to the table,
The vocal chorus that would meet,
Of mingled accents, harsh or sweet,
From every land and tribe, would beat,
  The polyglots of Babel.

Briton and Frenchman, Swede and Dane,
Turk, Spaniard, Tartar of Ukraine
  Hidalgo, Cossack, Cadi,
High Dutchman and Low Dutchman too,
The Russian serf, the Polish Jew,
Arab, Armenian and Manchoo,
  Would shout, "We know the lady!"

How many know what *cadi* means? I had to look it up.

In the North, Mrs. Stowe was praised for her fairness and impartiality, because she had represented the varying fortunes of Uncle Tom with various masters and localities; in the South she was condemned for exaggeration, slander, and falsehood. This is quite natural; had the Northern reviewers lived in the South, they would have said exactly what the Southerners said, and *vice versa.* Practically all our political, and many of our moral and religious opinions, are merely a matter of geography. This ought not to be so, but it is. Being so, we ought to have sympathy even with those we are compelled to fight. There were certainly just as sincere Christian ministers in the South as in the North, but they supported the institution of slavery, which to the Northerners seemed anti-Christian. Had the young men who fought for the Union been born and brought up in the South, they would all have fought against it. This is the reason why murderous animosities cool after many years, and we no longer call the Southerners traitors.

The reason why slavery had to go was be-because it was an anachronism. The spirit of the times was too much for it; not only could not this country exist half slave and half free, but slavery itself could not exist any longer in a country that called itself both civilised and Christian. Personally, although I am a Yankee of the Yankees, I have as much intellectual and moral respect for Southerners as for Northerners. The Southerners have never "repented" that they fought in the Confederate army; they are proud of it. They have statues to Confederate generals all over the South—why not? In following such leadership, they did what they sincerely believed to be their duty. It is a tragedy that abstract questions in politics and in morals have to be settled by bloody strife, but that is the method preferred by the majority of human beings; perhaps in the future men will find a better way, and perhaps not. To bring about such an improvement, there will have to be a prodigious rise in the general level of intelligence, and Christian precepts will have to be taken seriously.

To the statements that *Uncle Tom's Cabin* was a collection of lies, Mrs. Stowe issued a *Key,* which contained verifying footnotes to the material she used in her story. On this *Key* two observations may justly be made. The fact that special cases such as she cited had actually happened, did not prevent the book from being false. It was false as a picture of the general conditions of the slavery régime. On the other hand, the strength of her indictment consisted in this: her enemies could not deny that what she pictured might happen. Legree was a hideous exception, granted; but where he did flourish, there was no remedy. Suppose a slave-holder got drunk, and beat his slaves; he might regret his behaviour after he became sober, but that did not help his victim, nor was there any way in which he could be punished. Hopkinson Smith said that whenever a master was known to be cruel, his neighbours ostracised him; that may have acted as a deterrent in some cases, but there was no redress for those who had been injured. When you see a drunken man driving a horse, you respect the horse more than the man; but your respect does not help the horse.

The whole question, still hotly debated, as to whether the slaves were "better off" than their descendants in freedom, depends entirely upon whether you consider the blacks as human beings or as animals. A dog is better off in slavery than in freedom; nothing is more pitiable than a free dog. But men? There is a story told of a runaway slave in the 'fifties, who was asked several questions by a man in Ohio. "You were badly treated?" "Oh, no, master was very kind." "You were cold and hungry?" "No, indeed; we always had clothes to wear, good shelter, and good food." "Then you were a fool to run away." "Well, Sir, my place there is vacant; you can have it if you like it."

There is also a story told of a coloured man a few years ago, who being penniless and hungry, called at house after house in Boston, sent in his card, "Mr. Henry Brown," was received politely, but when he made his request, was with equal politeness, refused assistance. Finally, he happened to call at a place where a man lived who had moved up from the South; when this gentleman saw the negro in his drawing-room, he cried, "What the hell do you mean by sending in a visiting card, with *Mister* Brown on it? If you're hungry, go down into the kitchen, and the cook will give you anything you want." And Mr. Brown ejaculated, "Thank God! I've found one of my own people!"

The Southern people have as a rule treated the negroes more kindly and far more intimately than they are treated in the North; but when it comes to anything like political equality, the matter is not even debatable.

During the twenty-five years that I have

been teaching American Literature to college undergraduates, I have observed a remarkable change in the attitude of the students from the South. In the late 'nineties, when I first included *Uncle Tom's Cabin* as part of the required work, on which every member of the class had to write a critical theme, I remember what one warm-hearted young gentleman from a Southern State wrote: "After I had finished this book, I kicked it out of the room, kicked it down stairs, kicked it out of the dormitory, and shall never read it again." There were some other vigourous denunciations, which all seemed to me natural enough. But of late years the attitude has been so different, that it would often be impossible to tell by the theme what part of the country was represented by the writer. The young men from the South never believe that it is a fair picture of what slavery was; but they read it with interest, often with enthusiasm, and judge it fairly.

Was there a real Uncle Tom, and if so, who was he? In March 1903, the newspapers quite generally printed a dispatch with an illustration of the cabin, announcing that the original of Mrs. Stowe's portrait had recently died at Paint Lick, Kentucky, aged 111. His name was Norman Argo, and he belonged to General Samuel Kennedy, a planter of Howard county, and at one time a member of the State Legislature. It was announced also that Mrs. Stowe had obtained much material for her story from the Kennedy plantation.

One of my pupils at Yale in the class of 1905, Mr. Nathaniel B. Sewell, of Kentucky, wrote me the following statement:

> Half a dozen states have laid claim to the original Uncle Tom. Mrs. Stowe herself said that she had been impressed by many slaves possessing her hero's three most salient characteristics—devotion to master, honesty, and piety. But in Garrard County, Kentucky, where Mrs. Stowe frequently visited while her home was in Ohio, it is maintained to this day that her model hero was Uncle Tom Kennedy, the slave of a Bluegrass planter. Just fifty years after the publication of Uncle Tom's Cabin, I saw this original in Paint Lick, a rambling, Kentucky village, and certainly an odd little old negro he was. His garb consisted of coarse cowhide shoes without heels, trousers several inches too long, and goodness knows how many sizes too large, a coat large enough for an overcoat, a cotton-plaid shirt open at the collar, and a tall, bat-

tered white hat. His body was stooped and shrunken, and his withered face fringed with white whiskers; a striking picture of the humble, old-time darky. No one appeared to remember when he was otherwise than "Uncle Tom, and a mighty good old nigger." When spoken to by a white man, he removed the old white hat, bowed his head, and answered with great deference. His life had been a hard one, but he thought the Lord had been good to him in permitting him to live so long and in keeping his faith strong. He acknowledged the smallest favour, whether a kind word or a coin, with a fervent, "Gawd bless ye, Mas'r! Gawd bless ye!" He spoke with modest pride of Mrs. Stowe's visits to the home of his master long before the war. That she had been led by Providence to use him as an instrument for the deliverance of his race, he never doubted. But Uncle Tom's memory seemed decidedly treacherous. Sometimes he thought himself a hundred years old, again a hundred ten, then a hundred twenty-five. No one doubted his being the oldest man in the country round, and I heard no one accuse him of being a humbug.

Since the war, he had earned a scant living by doing odd jobs about the village, receiving occasional pieces of money from strangers and many kindnesses from the family and friends of his old master. In no sense does tradition make of him the remarkable character that Mrs. Stowe made of her hero; but I have heard since his death, which occurred several years ago, that the people, white and black, for many miles around, came to his funeral and scores of white people wept at his grave.

What is the literary value of *Uncle Tom's Cabin?* This is still a matter of hot dispute. In an interview in the *New York Sun,* 6 February 1898, Mr. Howells spoke of it in the highest terms. To him it was always a great novel. Professor Brander Matthews, who was born in New Orleans, has written of it with enthusiasm. Others can see in it only sensationalism, melodrama, sentimentality, and crass crudity.

To judge of the merits of the work, one should look at her other stories; some of them are worthless, but there are a few which show not a little creative art. I am certain that *Dred,* published in England as *Nina Gordon,* would have made a powerful impression if it had not been overshadowed by her masterpiece; and *Oldtown Folks* is a good novel. But the convincing proof of Mrs. Stowe's talents as a novelist is seen in the continued and world-wide popularity of *Uncle Tom's Cabin.* The issue is as dead as all questions that have been settled; nothing is more surely dead than an extinct controversy. Yet the book continues year after year to be a bestseller, both abroad and at home; young and old read it with interest and are often deeply affected. I believe it is a work of genius.

Whether truthful in detail or not, its spirit is true. It was written with absolute sincerity, with burning conviction; it came out of the tremendous heat caused by the fusion of passion and religion. It is aflame. You feel the fiery zeal of the author before you have read twenty pages, and there is no diminution, no cooling off.

She was a natural-born narrator. She had considerable power of invention; she described vividly; she visualised every scene.

There is enough humour to relieve the tension. A continuous strain of tragic feeling or of propaganda would have been unbearable. But Topsy is a creation that belongs immortally to the literature of comedy. She has contributed proverbs to the language. Indeed, creation of character is one of Mrs. Stowe's greatest gifts. Uncle Tom, Topsy, St. Clare, Aunt Ophelia, Simon Legree are real in the imagination, and cannot possibly be forgotten.

The dramatic skill shown in the book is notable. It was a long story and the terrible close is heightened by the scenes of contrast that preceded it. It is more untrue than anything in the book to say that it is an unrelieved picture of cruelty and oppression. Mrs. Stowe knew what she was about when she had Uncle Tom proceed from Shelby to St. Clare and from St. Clare to Legree. And the Legree episodes are even now terrifying. In him she created a monster who is by no means contemptible. The superstitious negroes have as high a respect for him today as they have for Satan. He is the antichrist, but he is to be taken seriously. He is utterly bad, but exceedingly formidable.

The pathos of the book is certainly overdone in the Little Eva scenes, but that was in the manner of Dickens, and quite fashionable in current fiction. Even as a small boy, I could not swallow Eva, and I did not have to swallow when I read of her exit. But the death of St. Clare is deeply affecting, and I can never read it unmoved. I detect no false note there. And the fatal effect of his accidental death on the fortunes of Uncle Tom is not over-emphasised.

Finally, it was a mark of intelligence on the part of the author to seize the exact moment. The time was precisely ripe. She expressed what thousands in the North had come to feel, and she converted thousands to her point of view. As a history of abolition sentiment it is not only a human but a historical document. In her preface she said, "It is a comfort to hope, as so many of the world's sorrows and wrongs have, from age to age, been lived down, so a time shall come when sketches similar to these shall be valuable only as memorials of what has long ceased to be."

The weaknesses of the book are only too apparent; nor would it be possible that a story written as blazing propaganda should have the flawless perfection of Turgenev or Hawthorne. In places the construction is as slipshod as the style; the dialect is absurd; the pathos is laid on too thick; there are too many plays to the gallery. If ever a book was certain of being dramatised, this was. But perhaps her very faults contributed to the effect, and the effect was what she was after. She obtained both fame and wealth; but when she was writing, she was not thinking of these things.

Towards *Uncle Tom's Cabin* we may take

the attitude taken by many scholars towards the Bible. Not every word in it is true, but it was inspired.

In a copy of the rare first edition in the Alldis collection in the library of Yale University, the following Scriptural passage appears in Mrs. Stowe's handwriting:

> The voice said Cry.—And he said, What shall I cry? All flesh is grass, and all the goodliness thereof is as the flower of the field. . . . The grass withereth, the flower fadeth; but the word of our God shall stand forever.

Perhaps that quotation explains the book's immortality.